CLEVELAND INDIANS
YESTERDAY & TODAY™

Phil Trexler
Foreword by Bob Feller
Preface by Rick Manning

WEST SIDE PUBLISHING

Phil Trexler is a writer for the *Akron Beacon Journal*. In his nearly 20 years of journalism experience, the native Clevelander has covered general news and local sporting events, including the 1995 and 1997 World Series and the 1997 All-Star Game. His work has garnered more than two dozen awards, and he has been a guest analyst for CNN, FOX News, NBC, and other broadcast news organizations.

Bob Feller has been the face of the Cleveland Indians for more than 70 years, making his big-league debut in 1936 at the age of 17. The fireballing right-hander struck out 2,581 batters in his 18 seasons as an Indian and collected 266 victories, despite the fact he spent 44 months in the U.S. Navy at the prime of his career. Feller pitched three no-hitters and played for nine American League All-Star Teams before being inducted into the National Baseball Hall of Fame in 1962. He currently resides in the Cleveland area and is a public relations executive for Ro-An-Fel, Inc.

Cleveland's first-round draft pick in 1972, **Rick Manning** played center field for the Indians from 1975 to 1983. Manning's stellar outfield play earned him a Gold Glove in 1976. Although he was traded to the Milwaukee Brewers during the 1983 season, he returned to the Indians in 1989 as a color commentator. Twenty years after calling his first game, Manning is still in the booth, adding color to 150 Indians games per year.

Consultant: Richard Johnson

Factual Verification: Karl Hente

Acknowledgments
Special thanks to Mark Rucker of Transcendental Graphics, John Horne of the National Baseball Hall of Fame Library, Russell Schneider, and Jane Martin. Also, special thanks to Bill Barrow, Special Collections Librarian at the Cleveland State University Library, and to Vern Morrison of the Digital Production staff at the Cleveland State University Library.

Front cover: **Ron Kuntz**

Back cover: **Diamond Images/Getty Images**

AP Images: contents, 28 (right center), 31 (left), 36, 42 (right), 43 (left), 44 (bottom left), 46 (right), 48 (right), 49 (top), 52 (bottom), 53 (left), 54 (top left & bottom right), 57 (top), 59 (top), 69, 70, 73 (top), 76 (top), 79, 82 (bottom), 86 (bottom), 87 (top), 88, 92, 94, 99 (top right & bottom right), 101, 103 (top center), 112 (top), 113 (top), 114, 115, 118 (bottom), 119, 122 (top), 123, 126, 129 (top right & bottom left), 130, 131, 133 (right), 135 (top & right center), 137 (center); **Doug Brooks Collection:** 34 (top right); **Brown Brothers:** 29 (left center); *Cleveland Plain Dealer:* 17 (left center); **Cleveland Press Collection, Cleveland State University Library:** 19 (bottom), 24 (right), 27 (left), 28 (top right), 34 (bottom), 67 (top left), 73 (bottom), 75 (left), 76 (bottom), 82 (top); Herman Seid, 42 (left); Paul Tepley, 91 (bottom); Paul Toppelstein, 80; ©**Corbis:** Bettmann, 25 (top right), 45 (left center & bottom right), 47 (top), 52 (top), 54 (bottom left), 55 (top left), 81 (top), 83 (top left), 85 (bottom right), 93; Gunther/epa, 125; **Courtesy Bob Feller:** 6; **Getty Images:** 10 (left), 11, 13 (bottom), 19 (top right), 31 (right), 39, 83 (top right), 104 (top), 105 (top), 118 (top), 124 (right), 129 (right center), 132 (top), 134 (top), 135 (bottom center); AFP, 103 (right), 104 (bottom), 105 (bottom), 106, 107 (top & right), 110, 111, 112 (bottom), 120 (bottom), 121 (top), 127; Diamond Images, 86 (top); MLB Photos, 12 (left), 20 (left), 62, 83 (bottom), 89 (top), 90 (right), 91 (top), 120 (top); *Sports Illustrated*, 74 (top left), 77 (right), 97 (top left), 98; Time Life Pictures, 40, 41 (top left), 47 (bottom), 64, 71 (left); **Richard Johnson Collection:** 22, 46 (left); **Library of Congress:** 14 (left), 15 (top), 17 (bottom), 27 (right), 43 (right); **National Baseball Hall of Fame Library, Cooperstown, N.Y.:** contents, 3, 10 (right), 12 (right), 16 (top left & top right), 17 (right center), 20 (right), 28–29 (bottom), 29 (right), 30 (left), 32 (left), 35 (top right), 37 (right), 38 (right), 44 (bottom right), 61 (top center & right), 68 (bottom), 71 (right), 85 (top right), 102 (right); Milo Stewart, 45 (top left); **Courtesy Rick Manning:** 8; **PIL Collection:** 13 (top), 15 (bottom), 17 (top), 18, 19 (top left), 21 (bottom), 24 (left), 25 (bottom), 26 (bottom), 28 (top left), 30 (right), 33 (left), 34 (top left), 35 (top left & bottom), 38 (left), 41 (top right & bottom), 44 (top left & top right), 45 (top right), 48 (left), 49 (bottom), 50, 51, 55 (top center & top right), 56, 58, 59 (bottom), 60, 61 (top left), 63, 65, 66, 67 (top center, top right, right center & bottom left), 72, 74 (top right, right center & bottom right), 75 (bottom right), 78, 81 (bottom), 84, 85 (bottom left), 87 (bottom), 89 (bottom), 95, 96, 97 (top right), 100 (left), 102 (left), 107 (left center), 108 (top left), 116 (top left, top right & bottom right), 117 (bottom right), 121 (bottom), 122 (bottom), 124 (left), 128, 129 (top left & bottom center), 133 (left), 134 (bottom), 135 (bottom left), 136 (left, center & right), 137 (top), 139 (right); **Mark Rucker Collection, Transcendental Graphics:** 14 (right), 16 (bottom), 21 (top), 23, 25 (top left), 26 (top), 29 (top), 32 (right), 33 (right), 37 (top), 53 (right), 54 (top right), 55 (bottom left), 57 (bottom); **Phil Trexler Collection:** 75 (top right), 77 (left), 85 (top left), 90 (left), 97 (bottom), 99 (left), 103 (top left), 108 (top right, bottom left & bottom right), 109, 113 (bottom), 117 (top left & top right), 136–137 (bottom), 140, 141; **WireImage:** 100 (right); **ZUMA Press:** Cal Sport Media, 138 (right); Albert Dickson/*Sporting News*, 116 (bottom left), 132 (bottom); Icon SMI, 138 (left); Louis Lopez/Cal Sport Media, 139 (left); *Sporting News*, 68 (top)

Photography: Fuchs and Kasperek Photography; PDR Productions, Inc.

Front Cover Colorizing: Lisa O'Hara, Wilkinson Studios, Inc.

Yesterday & Today is a trademark of Publications International, Ltd.

West Side Publishing is a division of Publications International, Ltd.

Copyright © 2009 Publications International, Ltd. All rights reserved. This book may not be reproduced or quoted in whole or in part by any means whatsoever without written permission from:

Louis Weber, CEO
Publications International, Ltd.
7373 North Cicero Avenue
Lincolnwood, Illinois 60712

Permission is never granted for commercial purposes.

ISBN-13: 978-1-4127-1656-7
ISBN-10: 1-4127-1656-X

Manufactured in China.

8 7 6 5 4 3 2 1

Library of Congress Control Number: 2008936552

Reporters surround player-manager Lou Boudreau as he celebrates the Cleveland Indians' victory over the Boston Braves in the 1948 World Series. At the time, fans thought they were greeting a new baseball dynasty, but the Tribe hasn't tasted championship glory since, despite getting close in recent years.

Contents

Nap Lajoie — Page 10

Tris Speaker — Page 20

Max Patkin — Page 46

Foreword 6

Preface 8

CHAPTER 1
Major-League Beginnings: Late 19th Century–1919 10
The Seeds Are Planted 12
Napoleon's Reign 14
Baseball's Cozy Palace 15
Indian Memories 16
Shoeless Joe's Cleveland Years 18
Gone Too Soon 19
The Eagle Lands in Cleveland 20

CHAPTER 2
Tragedy and Triumph: 1920–1935 22
Tragedy in New York 24
Dirty Sox Suspended—Tribe Cleans Up ... 25
Best of Nine: Cleveland Takes the Title ... 26
Indian Memories 28
Short-Lived Success 30
Spoke's Last Hurrah 31
Depression-Era Heroes 32
Indian Memories 34
Lakefront Property 36

CHAPTER 3
The Golden Age: 1936–1954 38
Rapid Robert Arrives................ 40
There *Is* Crying in Baseball 42
Country Came First 43
Indian Memories 44
Bill Veeck's Tribal Revival 46
Doby Follows Jackie, Leads AL 48
The Boy Wonder 50
Indian Summer, 1948 51
Tribe on Top 52
Indian Memories 54
The One and Only Satchel Paige 56
The Second-Place Skipper 57
The Evolution of Chief Wahoo 58
Voices of the Tribe 59
The Big Four Fall Short 60

CHAPTER 4
The Rocky Road: 1955–1968 62
Woulda, Coulda, Shoulda 64
Indian Memories 66
Score Goes Down................... 68
Planet Piersall 69
Indian Giver 70
Rock Rolled Out of Town 71
Red Ink and Empty Seats 72
Exclusive Club Gets Early Addition..... 73

Indian Memories 74
The Cuban Whirlwind 76
Sudden Rise, Sudden Fall 77

CHAPTER 5
The Lost Tribe: 1969–1993 78
Drawing in Fans 80
Lights Out 81
The Nick of Time 82
The Ones Who Got Away 83
Indian Memories 84
Spit and Polish 86
Ten-Cent Beers and Five-Cent Heads 87
Cleveland Makes History—Again 88
Andre the Giant 90
From Super Joe to Average Joe 91
Perfecto! 92
Baseball Resurrected in Cleveland 93
Captains of the Titanic 94
One-Man Wrecking Crew 95
Indian Memories 96
Spring Training Tragedy 98
Goodbye, Muny 99

CHAPTER 6
Tribe Turnaround: 1994–2000 . . . 100
Cleveland's Crown Jewel 102
Surly Slugger 104
The Fast Track to Stardom 105
Pennant Fever: An Epidemic Returns 106

Indian Memories 108
Tribe Pride 110
O's No! 111
Defeat from the Jaws of Victory 112
Magic Man 114
The Brain Trust 115
Indian Memories 116
Still No Cigar 118
Man, Oh, Manny 120
This Second Baseman Second to None . . . 121
The Beat Goes On 122
Big Bucks and Big Expectations 123

CHAPTER 7
Ready for Glory: 2001–Today 124
Last Gasp 126
The Thomenator 127
Indian Memories 128
The Man with the Plan 130
Left-handed Leviathan 131
Pronk Power 132
Face of the Franchise 133
Too Close for Comfort 134
Indian Memories 136
Still Waiting 138

CHAPTER 8
Leaders and Legends 140

Index 143

Frank Robinson — Page 88

Jacobs Field — Page 101

Grady Sizemore — Page 133

Foreword

Bob Feller

If the statue of me outside the main gate at Progressive Field could speak, it would tell you that I, Robert William Andrew—best known as "Bob"—Feller consider myself a very fortunate man.

I'm fortunate in that I've spent most of my life wearing a Cleveland Indians uniform. Fortunate, too, because my parents, William and Lena Feller, encouraged me to dream of being a major-league baseball player from the time I was nine years old, when my father bought me my first baseball uniform. Dad also bought two gloves, one for me and a catcher's mitt for him, and he always made time to play catch with me on our farm in Van Meter, Iowa.

When I was in my early teens, I was good enough to play with older boys, and my dad cleared several acres of pasture and built our own field of dreams. Fifty-seven years later, that diamond became the model for the movie *Field of Dreams*. In 1934, a scout for the Indians, Cy Slapnicka, showed up at our field of dreams to watch our town team play. He said he wanted "to see the young fellow people say throws a baseball so fast the players on the other team can't hit it."

I was that "young fellow," and from that day on my favorite team was the Cleveland Indians.

I was only 16 years old and still in high school, but Slapnicka offered us a contract with the Indians. My "bonus" was a check for $1—which I still have on display in my Bob Feller Museum in Van Meter—and an autographed ball. Signing with the Indians instead of starting with a minor-league team was technically in violation of a major-league rule then in effect, and when it was brought to light, Commissioner Judge Kenesaw Mountain Landis threatened to void my contract. But my dad contended that a man's word was his bond, and he had given our word to Slapnicka. Consequently, Landis eventually backed down and allowed me to stay with the Indians.

I was still in high school in 1936 when the Indians brought me to Cleveland. I pitched in a couple of amateur games and then pitched three innings in an exhibition against the St. Louis Cardinals. I struck out eight of the nine batters I faced, and afterward a photographer asked Cardinals pitcher Dizzy Dean if he would pose with me.

Dizzy answered: "Why are you asking me? Ask the kid if he'll pose with me."

I won my first regular-season game on August 23, against the St. Louis Browns, 4–1. I struck out 15, one shy of the American League record at that time. It was the first of 570 games I would pitch for the Indians.

In my fifth start (on September 13), I broke the AL record by striking out 17 in a 5–2, two-hit victory over the Philadelphia Athletics. Two years later, on October 2, 1938, I set another new record with 18 strikeouts in a 4–1 loss to the Detroit Tigers.

Fortunately, my dad lived long enough to know that I fulfilled my dream—*our dream*, really—of becoming a major-league pitcher. He died in 1943, seven years after being diagnosed with brain cancer. Unfortunately, he did not live long enough to know that all the things he taught me would result in my becoming one of the game's most successful pitchers and a member of the Hall of Fame, which I was elected to in 1962.

I know that my parents also were proud of me on December 10, 1941, when I enlisted in the Navy three days after the Japanese bombed Pearl Harbor. I never discussed it with them because I knew they'd understand as long as it was something I felt I should do, which I did, even though I was at the peak of my career. I had been a 20-game winner for three consecutive seasons. It's been estimated that I could have won 100 or more games during the nearly four seasons I was in the Navy, and maybe I would have. That would have given me 360 or 370 victories, making me one of the four or five winningest pitchers in the history of baseball.

I've made lot of dumb decisions in my life, but joining the Navy after Pearl Harbor was not one of them. I'll always be proud that I did. I served 44 months aboard the USS *Alabama* as a chief petty officer and gun captain. Our battleship earned five campaign ribbons and eight battle stars, and it was credited with 22 "kills" (Japanese planes shot down).

I look back on my career with a great deal of pride and few regrets. I played with and against some of baseball's best players. I'm particularly proud to have been in the game when the so-called "color barrier" was broken, enabling me to be a teammate of two truly great players of any color: Satchel Paige and Larry Doby. I'm also proud to say that both Paige and Doby are still teammates of mine—and deservedly so—in the Hall of Fame.

As the Indians' unofficial goodwill ambassador, I enjoy my interaction with the fans and my participation in the Indians' annual Fantasy Camp. And when people ask me if, at my age, I can still throw hard, I tell them yes. I still throw as hard as I ever did...but for some reason the ball doesn't go as fast as it used to.

Something else that fans want to know, and think I can answer for them, is how close our team is to getting back to the World Series. I can only tell them to keep the faith, as I do, and that I hope I live long enough to see it happen.

But frankly, I hope they do it soon. At my age I can't wait a whole lot longer.

Bob Feller

Preface

I first came to Cleveland in 1972, when I was just 17 years old. Fresh out of LaSalle High School in Niagara Falls, New York, I had nothing more than a couple of dollars in my pocket and a dream of playing professional baseball.

The Indians drafted me in the first round as a shortstop—it wasn't until after my first few weeks in single-A Reno that I moved to the position I played for the remainder of my career. In fact, in my final game at shortstop I made four errors. That's when my visionary manager decided to end my infield career and introduce me to the outfield.

I played two years in the Indians farm system before being called up to the major leagues in 1975. The moment I knew I had finally made it to the bigs was when our manager homered on Opening Day of my rookie season. The legendary Frank Robinson was player-manager for the Indians, and he was definitely one of the first major-leaguers to influence me. Playing alongside a Hall of Famer like Frank Robinson every day helped develop me as a fielder. Because I was constantly challenged to meet my defensive potential, I was awarded a Gold Glove in just my second season.

Despite some personal success, the 1970s were a tough time for Cleveland baseball, not only for fans but also for players. We didn't win a lot of games, but my teammates and I will always have a place in our hearts for the Tribe fans who supported us day in and day out at old Cleveland Municipal Stadium. We played hard, we always tried to have fun, and our lineups were never shy of talented players. The Indians of those years consisted of ballplayers like Buddy Bell, Ray Fosse, Boog Powell, Gaylord Perry, Duane Kuiper, and Andre Thornton, and I know we gave Cleveland the best show that we could. We may not have won very often, but every now and then we gave the fans something spectacular to remember.

Dennis Eckersley's no-hitter in 1977 was the first truly memorable game I played in. Eck was only 22 when he no-hit the Angels, but he dominated that game like the Hall of Famer we all knew he would eventually become. I thought it would be impossible to see someone top Eck's gem, but just four years later, Len Barker took the mound and delivered a pitching performance that will never be surpassed.

May 15, 1981, is a date that will forever be tied to Cleveland baseball history because that's the day "Large Lenny" pitched nine perfect innings. I was playing center field that

Rick Manning

night and saw him effortlessly plow through 27 consecutive Toronto Blue Jays. When the last batter came to the plate, I had only one thought in my mind: Please hit it to me. The ball came in my direction, and I fielded the most significant fly ball of my life. Catching that final out of Lenny's perfect game was by far the most joy I ever felt on a baseball field. He made history that night, and I couldn't be more proud to have been a part of it.

At the beginning of the 1983 season, I was traded to the Milwaukee Brewers. I didn't want to leave Cleveland, but being traded is a part of the game, regardless of emotional ties. I finished my career playing the next five seasons in Milwaukee. I wasn't sure what I was going to do once I retired from the game but, as it turns out, my time with the Indians had barely begun.

Nowadays when a ballplayer's career is over, he usually goes into coaching or broadcasting. SportsChannel approached me in 1989 to do the color commentary for 11 Tribe games. I didn't have any experience in television, but I was told I didn't need any. However, TV seemed like a good way for me to stay in the game without having the demanding lifestyle of a coach. The next thing I knew, those original 11 games turned into a 20-year broadcasting career.

Being on TV the past two decades has allowed me to witness Indians success that I only imagined as a player. The ballclub's resurgence in the 1990s was unforgettable. The entire city was surrounded by an aura unlike anything I've ever seen. Season after season the teams managed to accomplish one incredible milestone after another. Omar Vizquel had nearly a decade-long dominance at shortstop, winning nine straight Gold Gloves. Sandy Alomar, Jr., had a storybook season in 1997 and was the hometown All-Star Game MVP in the same year we came within a single heart-wrenching game of winning the World Series. And for five seasons the fans sold out Jacobs Field for 455 consecutive games.

However, the one thing that was most personally gratifying was seeing my former teammates Mike Hargrove, Buddy Bell, and Toby Harrah lead the Tribe to the World Series and bring the first American League pennant to Cleveland in more than 40 years. This town will never forget the run that we had in the 1990s—it was long overdue and was something that Indians fans had been dreaming about for years.

I couldn't be happier with my role in the Indians organization today. I broadcast 150 Tribe games every season, serve on the board for Cleveland Indians Charities, and help run the successful Indians Fantasy Camp in the off-season. I have been fortunate to stay in baseball this long, and I couldn't have chosen a better city and ballclub for my journey. I have loved Cleveland since day one, and it will always be my home. Thank you, Cleveland, for making my baseball dreams come true. I hope to continue proudly serving you for many years to come.

Rick Manning

CHAPTER ONE

MAJOR-LEAGUE BEGINNINGS LATE 19TH CENTURY—1919

Early professional baseball's path through Cleveland was as circuitous and twisted as the crooked Cuyahoga. Haphazard teams in slapdash leagues brought fleeting success, but they also spawned plenty of growing pains and decisive failures. These early years defined Cleveland, an emerging international manufacturing mecca, as a major-league metropolis and forged a baseball identity.

Left: Clevelanders saw a contender at League Park with its newly christened Naps, a team that boasted the likes of 1903 AL batting champion Nap Lajoie (*second row from bottom, far right*), hard-hitting outfielder Elmer Flick (*bottom row, second from left*), and a 23-year-old pitching sensation named Addie Joss (*second row from top, second from right*). *Right:* During his career, Nap Lajoie won five batting titles, a Triple Crown, and the adoration of fans across the country, as he became baseball's first national superstar. Lajoie was inducted into baseball's Hall of Fame in 1937, along with two other Cleveland legends, Cy Young and Tris Speaker. *Opposite:* The 1890 Cleveland Spiders featured future Hall of Famer Cy Young (*middle row, third from left*), shortstop Ed McKean (*middle row, second from left*), and catcher Chief Zimmer (*middle row, second from right*), but the National League club wasn't ready for prime time just yet—they went 44–88 that season.

The Seeds Are Planted

Above: Bobby Wallace was a 20-year-old pitching prospect when he made his debut with the 1894 Spiders. After three mediocre seasons on the mound, he moved to third base and hit .335 and drove in 112 runs. The move allowed him to flash the leather that would eventually take him to Cooperstown. *Above right:* They might look calm here, but these Spiders dodged cabbages, apples, and rotten eggs tossed at them en route to Cleveland's first baseball championship, the 1895 Temple Cup. The Spiders won the best-of-seven matchup with the heavily favored Baltimore Orioles 4–1 in a series played in rowdy surroundings that were flush with alcohol and gambling.

Some came by foot, others by carriage—2,000 curious onlookers plunked down two bits each to witness Cleveland baseball history on June 2, 1869. There were no seats inside Case Commons, but that East Side diamond hosted Cleveland's first professional baseball team, the Forest Citys.

The rogue bunch of amateurs and pros took the field against the big-spending, well-established Cincinnati Red Stockings. The local nine was tarred-and-feathered 25–6, but Cleveland started developing into a fanatic baseball town.

The Forest Citys and nine other teams formed America's first professional baseball league, the National Association of Professional Base Ball Players, or the National Association, in 1871. Season tickets for the Cleveland club were $6; for $10, a man could bring his wife and park his carriage along the foul line to watch the games and Cleveland's first star, catcher Jim "Deacon" White. Unfortunately, financial instability and mismanagement, low attendance, player and fan rowdiness, gambling, and contract-jumping crippled the National Association. Cleveland left the NA after only two seasons, and the league folded in 1875.

William Hollinger revived pro ball in Cleveland four years later. He collected 10 players, including "drop ball" artist Jim McCormick and slugging catcher Doc Kennedy, for a new National League team that sportswriters called the Blues. Short on money and long on player defections, the venture ended after six uneventful seasons at tree-lined Kennard Street Park.

Local streetcar tycoon Frank Robison and his brother Stanley resurrected the Blues in 1887. Although the Blues started in the "beer and whiskey" American Association, they moved to the more stable NL two years later. Expectations weren't terribly high for that 1889 NL season. Part-owner George W. Howe took one look at the squad of wiry-legged, skinny-armed ballplayers and groaned, "They're nothing more than spiders."

The Cleveland Spiders were born.

The Spiders played their 1891 home opener at Robison's new 9,000-seat League Park at East 66th Street and Lexington Avenue. Pitching that May 1 afternoon was a local farmer's son, Denton True Young, who baffled Cincinnati en route to a 12–3 Cleveland victory. The kid's sizzling fastball earned him the nickname Cyclone. Later, they just called him Cy.

Young and sluggers Jesse "The Crab" Burkett and Ed McKean led the Spiders to the city's first championship, the Temple Cup, in 1895. But in 1899, Robison, thinking he could make more money with the St. Louis NL team he owned, moved the Spiders' best players to Missouri. Cleveland went 20–134 and finished 84 games out of first place. This team was such an embarrassment that it played the entire second half of its schedule on the road. The National League disbanded the Spiders at the end of the season.

This freefall prepared fans for what awaited them as the century flipped and Cleveland found a new home in the outlaw American League.

Jessie "The Crab" Burkett didn't smile much, if ever. But the slugging outfielder's hitting displays made Spiders fans joyous. From 1893 to 1898, Burkett never hit worse than .341, and he twice led the NL in hitting.

The Original Cleveland Indian

Louis Sockalexis was an immensely talented prospect who hit .338 as a rookie for the 1897 Cleveland Spiders. However, he was also a Penobscot Indian, so many white fans taunted him mercilessly. Sockalexis couldn't win them over because his game had two flaws: curveballs and whiskey. Alcoholism and an ankle injury caused by a jump from a brothel window put Sockalexis out of the game at 28 after only three seasons. He died on December 24, 1913. Two years later, Cleveland needed a new nickname for its team, and "Indians" (an informal nickname for the Cleveland squad when Sockalexis played) won a newspaper poll and was adopted.

For decades, the story was that "Indians" was chosen to honor Sockalexis, but by 2000, the team's media guide emphasized the popular vote, which may have been influenced by the Boston Braves' 1914 World Series victory.

Napoleon's Reign

On June 4, 1912, in a pregame celebration at League Park commemorating the tenth anniversary of Nap Lajoie's first game in Cleveland, fans presented the second baseman with a nine-foot horseshoe-shape floral arrangement that shimmered with 1,000 silver dollars. The bounty is worth about $22,000 in today's money.

*I*f given the chance, Clevelanders may have voted to change their city's name in his honor. As it was, they renamed their baseball team after Napoleon "Nap" Lajoie.

Lajoie was a graceful second baseman for the Philadelphia Athletics who won the American League Triple Crown in 1901 with a .426 batting average, which remains a league record. Lajoie was so feared, he once drew an intentional walk when the bases were loaded.

Lajoie ended up in Cleveland almost by accident. The A's had signed him away from the National League's Philadelphia Phillies with a contract that paid him substantially more than the NL's $2,400-per-year salary cap. The Phillies protested the player raid, and the Pennsylvania Supreme Court ruled Lajoie had to return to the Phillies. The ruling was only enforceable in Pennsylvania, so A's owner Connie Mack traded Lajoie to Cleveland in 1902 to keep him in the AL.

Cleveland fans were so overjoyed with the superstar's arrival that they voted to change the team's nickname from the Bronchos to the Naps.

"Lajoie was the Babe Ruth of our day," Cy Young would recall. "The kids followed him around, just as they hung after Ruth."

Lajoie took the AL batting title in 1903 and 1904, but the Naps finished no better than third, so manager Bill Armour was fired and Lajoie was named skipper for the 1905 season. The dual role hurt his hitting, so Lajoie resigned as manager in the middle of the 1909 season. His batting stroke returned, and he was within a percentage point of snatching the 1910 batting title from Ty Cobb in a hotly contested race.

Lajoie would remain in Cleveland through 1914, but he never led the Naps to the pennant. At 40, he went back to the Athletics, leaving the Cleveland club in need of a new nickname.

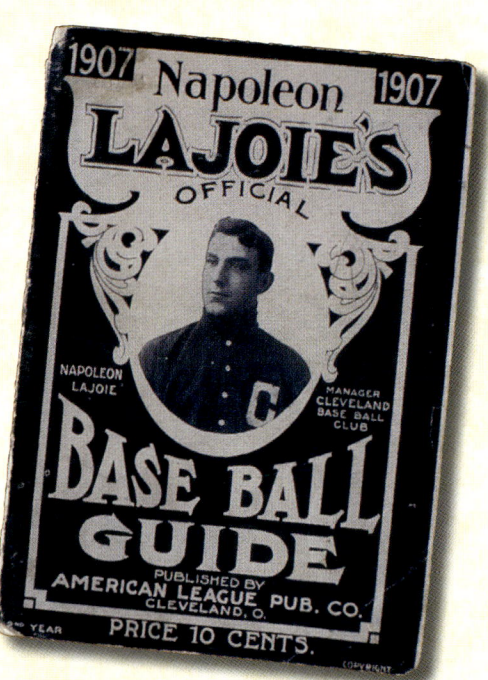

Years before Babe Ruth, American baseball found a superstar in Nap Lajoie. Cleveland's player-manager was so popular that the American League published *Napoleon Lajoie's Official Base Ball Guide* for the 1907 season.

Baseball's Cozy Palace

By 1910, Cleveland was the seventh-largest city in America, a melting pot of immigrants who brought plenty of muscle, found regular paychecks, and thirsted for entertainment. Baseball was the best show in town, but the rickety, wooden, 9,000-seat League Park was no longer a suitable stage for a ballclub worth watching. It was time for an upgrade.

Concrete and steel replaced the battered pine grandstand. Box seats were bolted in, and hard benches were pried out. When the work was done, 21,000 fans could watch from two decks that wrapped around the infield. But the expansion didn't diminish League Park's intimacy or its odd-shape outfield, which was squeezed in the middle of an East Side neighborhood at East 66th Street and Lexington Avenue. Left field was 385 feet from home plate, the corner just left of center was 505 feet deep, but right field was an inviting 290 feet from the dish.

Kids manned the giant green scoreboard in center field. Other children chased balls that bounced on Lexington after flying over the towering right field wall. The youngsters exchanged them for a free ticket.

Oh, that wall. As much as it enticed batters, it tormented pitchers and right fielders. After the renovation, it was 20 feet of concrete without padding. Above that hung a 20-foot chicken-wire extension supported by steel beams. Few could predict a ball's bounce off the short porch as singles caromed off for extra bases. "Wall Ball" as it was called, would be played in these goofy confines until September 21, 1946.

Smack-dab in the middle of Cleveland's Hough neighborhood sat the inviting confines of League Park. The park featured a right-field wall just 290 feet from home plate. Fans were so close to the field, they could almost hear the tobacco being chewed.

Ty Cobb (*left*) and Joe Jackson

What Could Have Been

League Park could have been home to a dream team outfield of "Shoeless" Joe Jackson, Tris Speaker, and Ty Cobb. Before the 1908 season, the Detroit Tigers offered to trade Cobb to the Naps for oft-injured outfielder Elmer Flick, who had won the 1905 AL batting title but was fading fast. Detroit wanted to rid itself of the talented but ornery Cobb, who at 21 had just won his first batting title. Cleveland passed on the deal to avoid upsetting the team chemistry. Speaker arrived from the Boston Red Sox in 1916, and Jackson spent 1910 to 1915 in the Forest City before being sold to the Chicago White Sox.

THE NATIONAL LEAGUE'S TOP TWO FINISHERS MET FOR THE TEMPLE CUP FROM 1894 TO 1897. THE SPIDERS PLAYED FOR THE CUP IN 1895 AND 1896, EACH TIME AGAINST THE BALTIMORE ORIOLES. THE SPIDERS WON IT ALL IN 1895 BUT WERE SWEPT 4-0 THE NEXT YEAR.

NATIVE OHIOAN CY YOUNG HAD WON 241 CAREER GAMES FOR THE SPIDERS BEFORE HIS CONTRACT WAS "ASSIGNED" TO OWNER FRANK ROBISON'S OTHER CLUB IN ST. LOUIS AFTER THE 1898 SEASON. THIS IS YOUNG'S JERSEY FROM HIS LAST YEAR AS A SPIDER.

BASEBALL HISTORIANS ARE STILL DEBATING WHO WON THE 1910 AL BATTING RACE BETWEEN CLEVELAND'S NAP LAJOIE AND DETROIT'S TY COBB. THE COMPETITION WAS SO CLOSE THAT BOTH RECEIVED ITS PRIZE: A CHALMERS AUTOMOBILE.

LOOKS ARE NOT DECEIVING. THIS COLLECTION OF RAG-TAG SPIDERS FROM THE INFAMOUS 1899 SEASON PLAYED AS BADLY AS THEY POSED FOR TEAM PICTURES. THE SPIDERS LOST 134 GAMES TO FINISH DEAD LAST, 84 GAMES OUT OF FIRST PLACE.

THE 1913 TEAM RELIED ON LEFT-HANDER VEAN GREGG, WHO WAS VOTED THE TEAM'S BEST SOUTHPAW IN A POLL CONDUCTED IN 1969. GREGG WON 20 OR MORE GAMES EACH SEASON FROM 1911 TO 1913.

WITH NAP LAJOIE GONE AFTER THE 1914 SEASON, CLEVELAND'S BALL TEAM NEEDED A NEW NAME. THE ORIGINS OF THE NAME "INDIANS" ARE STILL CLOUDED IN UNCERTAINTY, BUT THERE IS NO DOUBT THAT THIS CARTOON, WHICH APPEARED IN THE CLEVELAND PLAIN DEALER TO ANNOUNCE THE NEW NICKNAME, WOULD BE VERY CONTROVERSIAL TODAY.

THE 1916 INDIANS NEEDED ALL THE HELP THEY COULD GET, EVEN FROM A FOUR-LEGGED FRIEND. THAT YEAR'S TEAM PHOTO FEATURED LARRY, A BULL TERRIER THAT SERVED AS THE TEAM'S MASCOT AND PERFORMED TRICKS UNDER THE GUIDANCE OF POPULAR OUTFIELDER JACK GRANEY.

17

Shoeless Joe's Cleveland Years

Cleveland fans found a new idol with an endearing nickname in "Shoeless" Joe Jackson. Jackson hit a career-best .408 in 1911, thanks in part to League Park's right-field wall. Despite a .356 lifetime average, Shoeless Joe never won a league batting title.

His swing was so sweet—each smack of ball-meeting-bat so unique—even Babe Ruth was envious.

"I copied Jackson's style because I thought he was the greatest hitter I had ever seen, the greatest natural hitter I ever saw," Ruth said.

There were few who could compare to Joseph Jefferson Jackson. The promising yet raw outfielder from the backwoods of South Carolina was nicknamed "Shoeless Joe." Jackson signed with the Philadelphia A's, but he never played to his potential. Frustrated A's owner Connie Mack traded Jackson to Cleveland in 1910 for outfielder Bristol Lord—surely among the most one-sided deals in baseball history.

Jackson and his four-pound bat named Black Betsy went to work full time in Cleveland in 1911. He hit .408—setting a rookie record that still stands—as the Naps climbed from fifth to third place. However, Jackson was more than just a hitter. He brought speed and a rifle arm to League Park's right field, the perfect package to deal with the wall's wacky bounces.

With Nap Lajoie's skills fading, Shoeless Joe became Cleveland's star attraction, but the team wasn't good enough to pull fans into the park. Owner Charles Somers was nearly broke by 1915. To fend off creditors, Somers traded Jackson to the Chicago White Sox for three nondescript players and—more importantly—$31,500.

The penny-pinching move set Jackson on course with destiny. In 1921, he was one of eight White Sox banned for life from baseball for throwing the 1919 World Series. His career batting average of .356 ranks third all-time and remains the highest of any player not in the Hall of Fame.

Someone at Selz Shoes saw a good advertising gimmick in a famous ballplayer.

Gone Too Soon

His pitching motion, which featured a high-leg kick that pivoted his back to home plate, was unorthodox. The results were historic, yet sadly abbreviated.

Addie Joss debuted in 1902 as a spindly, 6′3″ right-hander who flung fastballs and curves with equal deftness. In his first game, the 22-year-old tossed a one-hit shutout against the St. Louis Browns. The win foreshadowed a career of dominance that led Joss to baseball's Hall of Fame.

"No name is more hallowed in Cleveland baseball memories than Joss's," wrote sportswriter Franklin Lewis in 1949. "He was, from the outset, a tremendous pitcher, a superior competitor, and a gentleman."

His greatness was on display during the 1908 pennant race. Matched up against Chicago ace Ed Walsh on October 2, Joss hurled a perfect game, at the time only the second one in modern (post-1900) baseball history.

A shocking decline would follow. Arm troubles limited him to 46 starts the next two seasons, and a bout with tubercular meningitis would keep him from the mound forever. He died on April 14, 1911, just two days after his 31st birthday.

A team made up of the very batters Joss baffled during his career—including Ty Cobb, Tris Speaker, and Eddie Collins—played the Naps in a benefit game for Joss's widow and their two children. The game, baseball's first all-star event, raised nearly $13,000.

Left: Addie Joss won 160 games in nine seasons for the Naps, compiling the second-best ERA ever (1.89) and completing 234 of his 260 starts. Joss entered the Hall of Fame in 1978, when the 10-season minimum induction requirement was waived. *Above:* In baseball's first all-star game, the AL's best played the Naps on July 24, 1911, before 15,270 fans at League Park with proceeds going to benefit Addie Joss's family. Ty Cobb, who wore a Cleveland uniform because his Detroit garb was lost en route, led the AL to a 5–3 win.

Rained Out

Cleveland had the 1908 pennant in its sight, and after Addie Joss's perfect game on October 2, the *Cleveland Plain Dealer* boldly predicted the Naps would win the league. But raindrops in Washington, D.C., washed away all hope of Cleveland's first AL flag.

The Naps and Tigers won 90 games each, but the Tigers played one fewer game because league rules dictated that an early season rainout in Washington did not have to be made up. The protests heard up and down Euclid Avenue would not sway AL President Ban Johnson. The Tigers finished a half-game ahead of the Naps and were off to the World Series.

The Eagle Lands in Cleveland

Charles Somers and his empty pockets left League Park's owner's box after a dreadful 1915 season that saw the Indians finish 44½ games out of first place. In was "Sunny Jim" Dunn, a transplanted Iowan who had earned his wealth partnering in railroads. With the help of investors, he bought the club and immediately embraced his newfound notoriety. Dunn was intent on rejuvenating baseball in Cleveland with a star attraction the way Somers had profited from the arrival of Nap Lajoie more than a decade earlier.

Tris Speaker, a gifted former MVP just entering his prime with the Boston Red Sox, would be that star, albeit a reluctant one.

Nicknamed "Spoke" and the "Gray Eagle" (for his prematurely silver hair), Speaker was a fleet-footed center fielder who was regarded as the best player in the American League. He was the centerpiece of the "Million-Dollar Outfield" that helped the Red Sox win the World Series in 1915.

"You can write Speaker down as one of the two models of ball-playing grace," legendary sportswriter Grantland Rice penned. "The other was Napoleon Lajoie. They made hard plays look easy."

Tris Speaker found plenty of gaps in the League Park outfield, which helped him stretch his frozen ropes into more doubles than anyone else has ever hit in major-league history.

Speaker is considered one of the best defensive outfielders in the history of baseball. He still holds the career record for outfield assists, with 449, despite the fact that his career ended more than 80 years ago.

Speaker is still considered one of the best defensive center fielders of all time. He played extremely shallow and dared batters to beat him deep. When they hit low line drives, he snagged them and doubled up runners who strayed too far from base. In fact, with 139, he is still the career leader in double plays by an outfielder. He even recorded six unassisted double plays as an outfielder in his 22 seasons.

Spoke's bat was among the best in baseball, even when his average *slipped* to .322 in 1915. That is when Boston offered him $9,000 to play in 1916—less than what he had made the year before. Spoke told management he would rather retire to his home in Hubbard, Texas, than play for such a paltry sum. It was $15,000 or nothing, he told them.

The Red Sox worked to exile him to Cleveland. After winning two World Series in four seasons with Boston, the hapless Cleveland club was hardly alluring to the 28-year-old star. Money, more specifically Boston's money, soothed the Gray Eagle's angst.

In what was hailed as baseball's first blockbuster deal, Cleveland sent pitcher "Sad" Sam Jones, infielder Freddie Thomas, and $55,000 to Boston. Cleveland also agreed to meet Speaker's salary demand. However, the Gray Eagle wanted $10,000 of the money Boston received. The cash had to come from Red Sox owners, he insisted.

Speaker got what he wanted, and Cleveland got its box-office draw. Spoke hit .386 and won the AL batting title during his first of 11 seasons as an Indian, and he would go on to hit .380 or better three more times. His .345 career batting average is sixth best in major-league history, and his 792 doubles top the list for career two-baggers.

But his lasting legacy along the shores of Lake Erie will be that he brought Cleveland its first championship.

Cleveland owner Sunny Jim Dunn had to dangle a lot of cash to convince Red Sox star outfielder Tris Speaker to leave Boston in 1916 and play for the struggling Indians. By the time this card came out in 1922, Speaker had paid huge dividends on Dunn's investment.

Young Goes Home

Long before Art Modell, there were the Robison brothers, Frank and Stanley, owners who turned the Cleveland Spiders into a National League laughingstock and moved Ohio hero Cy Young out of Cleveland.

After a 25-win season in 1898 and 241 career victories in Cleveland, Young was "assigned" to Robison's St. Louis team. Jim Hughey, a 24-game loser in St. Louis in 1898, was "assigned" to Cleveland. Young won 237 more games in St. Louis and Boston before returning home to Cleveland in 1909 and winning 19 games at age 42. Young retired after the 1911 season with 511 career wins, almost 100 more than his closest competitor. While Robison has become a historic footnote, baseball to this day honors each season's best pitchers with the Cy Young Award.

CHAPTER TWO

Tragedy and Triumph
1920–1935

Grand visions preceded the construction of Cleveland's mammoth Municipal Stadium. However, shortly after the lakefront park opened in 1932, its imposing size had players and fans longing for the quaintness of League Park. For 14 years, the Indians were a two-park team.

AFTER BACK-TO-BACK SECOND-PLACE finishes in seasons shortened by war and tough economic times, Cleveland fans were ready for that elusive World Series season. They had the league's best all-around player, center fielder Tris Speaker, who was now managing the club. They had hard-hitting catcher Steve O'Neill, scrappy shortstop Ray Chapman, and homegrown second baseman Bill Wambsganss. That up-the-middle strength backed up a deep pitching staff. All the pieces came together in 1920—a season that was memorable for great loss and great reward—but success didn't last.

Opposite: Elmer Smith hit 70 home runs in 10 major-league seasons, but none compares to his devastating grand slam against Brooklyn in Game 5 of the 1920 World Series. Smith's blast, which didn't produce a huge gathering around home plate, was a Series first.

Tragedy in New York

Ray Chapman's sudden death rocked Cleveland and the sport of baseball. Tribe fans by the thousands mourned with Tris Speaker and the rest of Chapman's teammates, while players around the league threatened to boycott playing against Yankees hurler Carl Mays, whose pitch killed the beloved shortstop.

Ray Chapman was a blue-collar gamer. From the shortstop position, he flashed a sure-handed mitt and a surefire arm. In the batter's box he was fearless and gritty. He worked to become a .300 hitter, and like Tris Speaker, Chapman was a tireless competitor, which endeared him to Cleveland fans. The Gray Eagle saw him as a son.

All that admiration made August 16, 1920, the darkest day in Indians history.

The Indians, in a tight pennant race with the Chicago White Sox and New York Yankees, were at the Polo Grounds for a series with the Yanks. On the mound for New York was Carl Mays, a gruff spitball artist who had a deceptive submarine delivery and a reputation for plunking a batter when necessary.

In the top of the fifth inning, Chapman dug his metal spikes into the batter's box, assuming his usual crouched stance over home plate. Mays whirled, and Chapman froze. Some said his cleats stuck in the soft dirt. Mays's fastball drilled Chapman's left temple, which was protected by only a simple cloth cap. The nauseating thud echoed as the young shortstop dropped to the ground.

By the next morning, Chapman—29 years old, newly married, and about to become a father—was dead. He remains the only major-league player ever to die as a result of an injury suffered in a game.

"It was the most regrettable incident of my career and I would give anything if I could undo what has happened," Mays said.

More than 2,000 people went to Chapman's funeral at St. John's Cathedral in Cleveland, and another 3,000 waited outside. Distraught by the tragedy, Speaker did not attend. A World Series now seemed irrelevant.

"So stunned was the Cleveland fandom by the death of its popular idol," a *Sporting News* writer opined, "that in the shadow of his loss, the sinking of the Indians in the pennant race has aroused little comment."

Clevelanders relied on their local newspapers to report any news of Chappie's death. His death, still the only fatality attributed to an on-field injury during a major-league game, pulled a dark curtain of community-wide gloom over the city for several days.

Dirty Sox Suspended—Tribe Cleans Up

The 1920 AL pennant race was as hot as the sun-baked aluminum slide at Euclid Beach Park. The Indians, Yankees, and the defending AL champion White Sox battled all summer for first place. Throughout the season, however, reporters flirted with rumors that several members of the White Sox had thrown the 1919 World Series to the underdog Cincinnati Reds. Scandal was about to rock the sport after baseball spent 30 years rebuilding its reputation.

AL President Ban Johnson confirmed the rumors in late September before second-place Chicago's three-game series in Cleveland. With 10 days left in the season, the Indians were clinging to a 1½-game lead. Chicago took two of three in Dunn Field (formerly known as League Park), winning the last game on a blast by former Indian Joe Jackson.

But Jackson and six other Sox would see their season and careers end three days later after they were suspended by their team and later banned from major-league baseball for life by Commissioner Kenesaw Landis (one player had already left the majors). The short-handed Chicago team went 3–2 the rest of the way while the Indians won six of their last eight games to take the pennant by two games. Despite Cleveland's 98–56 record, some considered the Tribe's first flag to be tainted by the Chicago suspensions.

Inset: Although history has recorded his surname many different ways, Stan Coveleski identified himself to sports fans across America in the 1920 World Series. He won three games while surrendering just two runs in 27 innings of work. He won 24 games that season and 215 in his Hall of Fame career. *Right:* Jim Bagby was Cleveland's ace in 1920, when he won a career-high 31 games. He capped his unforgettable season by winning Game 5 and becoming the first pitcher to hit a home run in the World Series.

Great When It Counted

No sportswriter bestowed "The Great One" on John Walter Mails—the brazen southpaw gave himself the nickname. The 25-year-old pitcher was already a journeyman when the Indians purchased his contract and his considerable ego from the minors a day after Ray Chapman's funeral. For six weeks in 1920, however, Mails lived up to the moniker. Mails went 7–0 in four September weeks, helping the Indians win their first AL pennant. "The Great One" continued his streak into October against Brooklyn, winning his only World Series start with a three-hit shutout of his former team. But Mails didn't deliver on the promise of 1920. His career ended in 1926 with a not-so-great combined record of 32–25.

Best of Nine: Cleveland Takes the Title

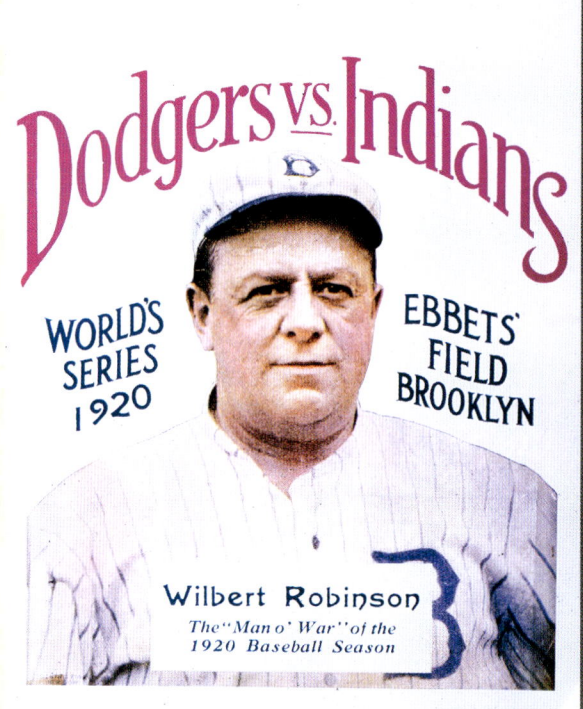

The favored Indians opened the 1920 World Series at Ebbets Field, where easy-going Brooklyn manager Wilbert Robinson reigned. His teams were alternately called the Dodgers and, in his honor, the Robins.

There was no time to breathe. The Indians had withstood a frantic summer-long pennant race. Ray Chapman's death was still fresh. Stan Coveleski, a 24-game winner, became a widower earlier in the season. All the Indians could do, as one newspaper headline urged, was carry on. And they did—all the way to the 1920 World Series.

It would be a best-of-nine matchup with the Brooklyn Dodgers (who were also called the Robins, after manager Wilbert Robinson), a veteran team that went 20–5 down the stretch to win its second National League pennant in five seasons. The Dodgers featured the NL's best pitching, which was backed by a formidable lineup led by future Hall of Famer Zack Wheat.

Cleveland's lineup was packed with .300 hitters and three sluggers who drove in more than 100 runs each. On the mound, the Indians boasted 31-game winner Jim Bagby and two 20-game winners in Coveleski and Ray "Slim" Caldwell.

There was, however, the matter of Joe Sewell, the shortstop who hit .329 after being called up from the minors in September. Sewell replaced Harry Lunte, who failed in his attempt to fill Chapman's shoes. Only special dispensation from Brooklyn allowed Sewell to play because he joined the team after the September 1 postseason-eligibility deadline.

Rube Marquard, a native Clevelander, was Robinson's surprise pick to take the mound for Game 1 in Brooklyn. Player-manager Tris Speaker gave reliable spitballer Coveleski the ball for the Tribe. There was only one more decision for the Indians to make: For the first

The 1920 Indians proved the old adage that pitching wins championships. Stan Coveleski (*front row, second from left*), Jim Bagby (*back row, far right*), and Ray Caldwell (*back row, second from left*) combined for 75 wins. Duster Mails (*back row, far left*) added seven down the stretch.

The eyes of the baseball world were on Cleveland and League Park, where Indians fans gathered for the city's first World Series. Without TV or radio, clamoring fans unable to see inside relied on the sounds of the crowd and word-of-mouth transmissions for game updates.

Game 5 Full of Firsts

Every World Series game is special, but few have been as historic as Game 5 of the 1920 title tilt.

Right fielder Elmer Smith sent a bases-loaded pitch over the right field wall in the first inning for the first World Series grand slam. In the fourth, Indians starting pitcher Jim Bagby became the first hurler to hit a homer in a Series game.

Second baseman Bill Wambsganss made the biggest news in the top of the fifth. Wamby snared Clarence Mitchell's line drive, stepped on second to double up Pete Kilduff, who was on his way to third, and then tagged Otto Miller, who was coming from first. It remains the only triple play in Series history.

Indians second baseman Bill Wambsganss poses with his unassisted triple play victims (*from left to right*): Pete Kilduff, Clarence Mitchell, and Otto Miller.

time since Chapman's death, the team donned black bands on the sleeves of their road-gray flannel jerseys.

The Dodgers got to Covey only once in Game 1, scoring a seventh-inning run on a double by Wheat and two groundouts. Backed by Steve O'Neill's two RBI, the Indians snatched the opener 3–1.

The Tribe's good fortune would be short-lived in Brooklyn, as the Dodgers would take a 2–1 Series lead back to Cleveland. But Speaker predicted the Indians would win the Series at Dunn Field.

"It's our home field, and our fellows are used to swinging for that right field wall," he said.

Dunn Field swelled with 25,734 fans for Cleveland's first Series game. Hundreds more stood along Lexington Avenue or around Public Square waiting for updates. Scalpers were getting six times the cost of a $5.50 seat. Businesses shut down as all eyes and ears were on the game.

Coveleski stymied Brooklyn in Game 4, again surrendering a single tally while Indian sluggers plated five runs on 12 hits. Game 5 was an 8–1 Cleveland rout, and Cleveland pitchers tossed shutouts in Games 6 and 7. Coveleski clinched the title in Game 7 with his third Series win.

More than 50,000 Clevelanders cheered their team a week later at a celebration in Wade Park. Cleveland stood atop the baseball world.

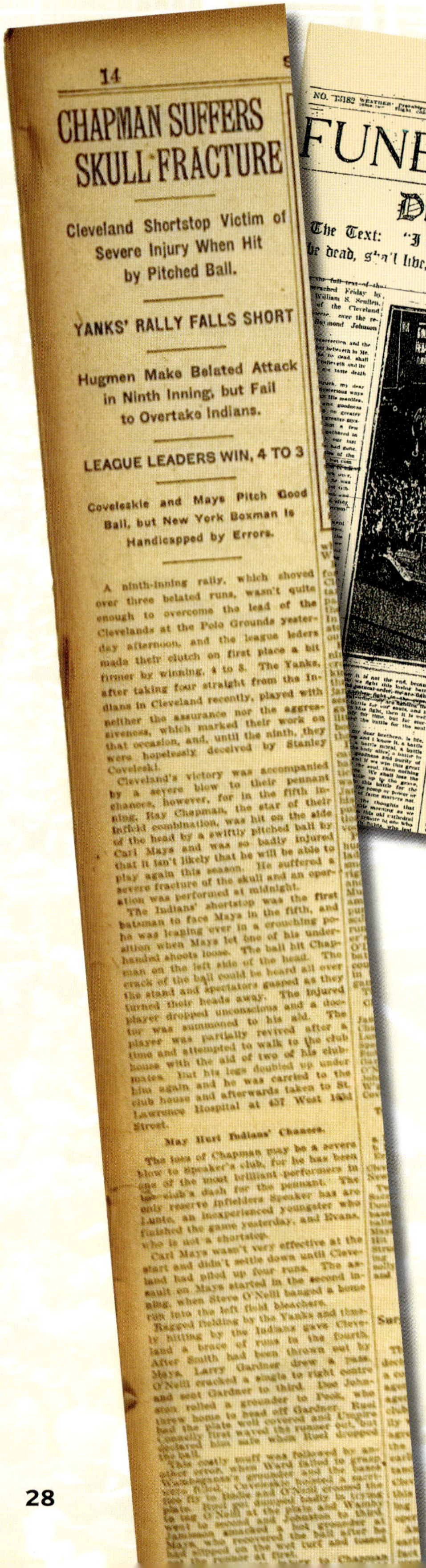

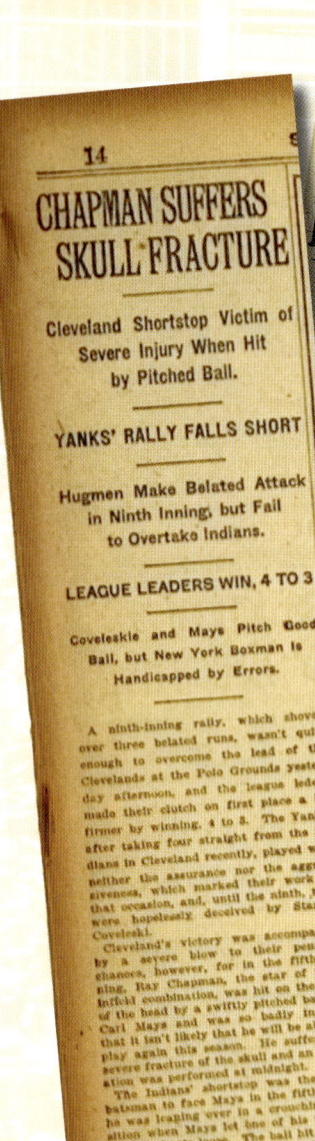

THE POLO GROUNDS IN NEW YORK WERE HUSHED WHEN INDIANS SHORTSTOP RAY CHAPMAN COLLAPSED AFTER CARL MAYS'S PITCH HIT HIM IN THE HEAD. CLEVELAND FANS FELT THE PAIN HUNDREDS OF MILES AWAY WHEN WORD CAME THAT CHAPMAN HAD DIED, AND THOUSANDS ATTENDED HIS FUNERAL.

TO THIS DAY, INDIANS FANS CONTINUE TO HONOR THE LIFE OF RAY CHAPMAN AS THEY LEAVE BEHIND BASEBALL MEMENTOS AT HIS GRAVE INSIDE LAKEVIEW CEMETERY ON THE EAST SIDE OF CLEVELAND.

JOE SEWELL DIDN'T MISS VERY OFTEN. IN FACT, HE STRUCK OUT ONLY 114 TIMES IN MORE THAN 7,000 CAREER AT-BATS, THE BEST MARK IN BASEBALL HISTORY. THE HALL OF FAMER WAS A CAREER .312 HITTER.

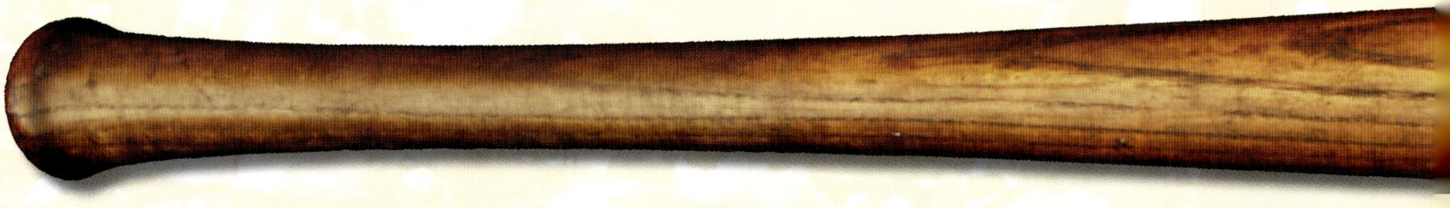

DESPITE RAY CHAPMAN'S DEATH, BASEBALL PLAYERS RESISTED DONNING HELMETS, INCLUDING THIS CLUNKY HEADGEAR. WEARING A BATTING HELMET DIDN'T BECOME MANDATORY FOR ALL PLAYERS UNTIL 1971, ALTHOUGH MANY PLAYERS WERE USING PLASTIC INSERTS IN THEIR CAPS IN THE 1950S.

TO ACCOMMODATE LARGER WORLD SERIES CROWDS AT LEAGUE PARK, OWNER SUNNY JIM DUNN HAD TEMPORARY BLEACHERS ERECTED IN RIGHT FIELD ALONG LEXINGTON AVENUE. BROOKLYN PITCHER RUBE MARQUARD TRIED TO CAPITALIZE, CAUSING A SENSATION WHEN CLEVELAND POLICE ARRESTED HIM FOR SCALPING HIS TICKETS.

IT WOULD BE A YEAR BEFORE FANS COULD HEAR A WORLD SERIES GAME ON THE RADIO, SO NEW YORKERS GATHERED BY THE THOUSANDS IN TIMES SQUARE TO CATCH GAME HIGHLIGHTS OF THE 1920 SERIES THROUGH TELEGRAPH WIRES.

Short-Lived Success

The 1921 Indians had a new look: The oversized "C" emblazoned on their jerseys was gone, replaced with the not-so-humble stitching "Worlds Champions." Misguided confidence was rampant in Cleveland. The champions had peaked and would make only two serious pennant runs over the next decade, falling short both times.

Tris Speaker was still tearing up AL pitching, but a knee injury and unfounded gambling allegations pushed him out of town after the 1926 season. The vaunted pitching staff that showed so much promise during the World Series withered. But most of all, baseball was changing; the dead-ball era of contact hitting, basestealing, and pitching was fading away. Home runs were all the rage. The Indians, meanwhile, stayed loyal to their small-ball style. The decision proved costly as the Roaring '20s roared by.

Still, there were hints of brilliance. George Burns, reacquired in a deal with Boston for Bill Wambsganss and Steve O'Neill, was the AL's most valuable player in 1926, knocking in 114 runs and rapping 64 doubles while hitting .358. But Burns was out of baseball three seasons later, washed up at age 36.

Lew Fonseca won the 1929 batting crown, hitting .369 while playing every infield spot. Fonseca survived scarlet fever in the off-season, but he was injury prone and was out of Cleveland by 1931. Charlie Jamieson, a throw-in from the 1919 Braggo Roth trade with the Athletics, was a perennial .300 hitter and a fan favorite.

From the bump, Joe "Lefty" Shaute and George Uhle would try to carry the pitching staff as Jim Bagby, Ray Caldwell, and Stan Coveleski burned out. Shaute was a one-season wonder, winning 20 games in 1924. Uhle, a Cleveland sandlot star nicknamed "The Bull," was a force on the mound and in the batter's box. He twice led the AL in wins and had a career batting average of .289.

But the pieces never became a whole. Around the corner lay another decade of promising talent and wasted hope.

When he wasn't fighting an injury, infielder Lew Fonseca was among the best pure hitters in the AL. He hit a league-best .369 in 1929, the only season in Cleveland in which he played more than 112 games.

First baseman George Burns hit .300 for the Indians in the 1920 World Series but was traded to Boston two years later. He returned to Cleveland in 1924 and won the 1926 MVP Award, hitting .358 and a then-record 64 doubles.

Spoke's Last Hurrah

By 1926, most of the championship team's stars were gone. Owner "Sunny Jim" Dunn had been dead since 1922, leaving his wife, Edith, in charge of the franchise. The legendary Tris Speaker was still with the club and was coming off an injury-shortened but successful campaign that saw him hit a career-best .389. However, he was 38—not exactly the golden age for professional athletes.

Dunn Field attendance was tumbling as badly as the Indians in the AL standings. Following a June swoon that saw the Indians plummet to fifth, 13 games behind the Yankees, another second-division season seemed likely in the summer of 1926.

Out of nowhere came the charge—one final run for old Spoke.

Pitcher George Uhle would finish with an AL-best 27 wins. Lefty Shaute and Dutch Levsen backed him up with 14 and 16 wins, respectively. Levsen even won both ends of a doubleheader against Boston, throwing two complete games. First baseman George Burns had an MVP season with a .358 average and 114 RBI. Shortstop Joe Sewell hit .324 and struck out just six times. Sewell, a future Hall of Famer, also continued his streak of 1,103 games without a day off.

Homer Summa, while not the power hitter his name suggests, hit .308, and Charlie Jamieson was his usual steady self, hitting .299. The team, however, was powerless, finishing dead last in home runs with 27. The Yankees would clobber 121.

Yet in September, the "Punch-n-Judy" Indians got themselves within 2½ games of the Bronx Bombers. Uhle pulled the trick in unlikely fashion, intentionally walking light-hitting Yankee shortstop Mark Koenig to get to the mighty Babe Ruth with two on and two outs. The Bambino had struggled all season against Uhle, and he struck out on a knee-high curveball.

The Indians could get no closer and finished second, three games out. The miracle run ended, as did Speaker's career in Cleveland.

The Gray Eagle looked grayer during spring training in 1926, but Tris Speaker managed to hit .304 as the Indians made one last run at the pennant. In the off-season, the Indians released Speaker as their player-manager amid gambling allegations that proved unfounded.

Speaker proved still popular when he returned to Cleveland in 1927 as a member of the Washington Senators. Fans honored their hero with Tris Speaker Day and bestowed gifts that included a horseshoe flower bouquet from Cleveland's policemen and firefighters.

Depression-Era Heroes

Clevelanders stood in line, not for Indians tickets but for soup and bread as the Great Depression bore down on the manufacturing city. Unemployment surged, businesses shuttered, and mortgages went unpaid.

Times had changed in a crash. Baseball as a business needed a response to survive.

Players, managers, and front-office staff saw their salaries slashed. In 1933, Indians owner Alva Bradley, who took over the club in 1927, cancelled radio broadcasts in a ploy to draw fans back to the park. But the team offered little distraction to harsh reality, finishing third, fourth, or fifth from 1930 to 1939. Attendance in Cleveland and around baseball dipped as fans bought essentials, not tickets, peanuts, or Cracker Jack.

General Manager Billy Evans searched for stars to revive the team. His finest find was Earl Averill, but for a while, it seemed the GM was alone in his admiration of the undersized outfielder.

"You certainly picked out a midget," Bradley told Evans.

"Yeah, but wait until you see him stripped down," Evans replied.

Underneath the flannel uniform, the 5'9" Averill was pure beef, with a nickname of "Rock." Averill homered in his first at-bat en route to a team-record 18 homers his rookie season in 1929. Rock made six All-Star teams during his 10 years in Cleveland and hit .318 over his 13-year Hall of Fame career. It would be six decades before an Indian eclipsed Averill's 226 career home runs.

From the Cleveland sandlots, Evans unearthed outfielder Joe Vosmik, who was dubbed the "Blond Viking" for his dashing good looks. Vosmik hit .300 or better in four of his six full seasons as an Indian (1931–1936).

Powerful left-handed slugger Hal Trosky wreaked havoc on League Park's inviting right-field porch when he arrived for his first full season in 1934. His 1936 season still ranks as one of the best in team history: 42 homers, 162 RBI, and a .343 batting average. Blinding migraines took a toll on the big man's game, and he was done playing in Cleveland by the time he was 28.

Staring down hitters with his steely blue eyes was intense pitcher Wes Ferrell. From 1929 to 1932, he won 20 games or more each

No Indians pitcher of the early 1930s was mightier or more fiery than right-hander Wes Ferrell (whomever misspelled his name on this photo probably felt his wrath). He won 20 or more games every year from 1929 to 1932.

Chief Wahoo in the 1930s was a far cry from the image that has been marketed to millions over the past few decades.

Mel Harder, with his stone-cold game face, arrived in Cleveland as an 18-year-old prospect in 1928. Nicknamed "Chief," Harder would pitch as an Indian until 1947 and then coach with the team through the 1963 season. His No. 18 is retired in Cleveland.

Earl Averill, nicknamed the "Earl of Snohomish," played parts of 11 seasons with the Indians and was named to six AL All-Star teams. He hit .318 over his career, but Averill never won a batting title—even his .378 mark in 1936 fell short.

season. In a shortsighted move, the Indians traded Ferrell to the Red Sox in 1934 for cash and two nondescript players. He went on to have two more 20-win seasons in Boston.

Mel Harder was, at least in temperament, the anti-Ferrell. The Chief stood as stoic as the Terminal Tower, winning 223 games as a career-long Indian, playing from 1928 to 1947.

Right-hander Johnny Allen was another personality pistol. He went 35–11 in his first two seasons in Cleveland, the highlight being a 15-game winning streak in 1937 that not even an appendectomy could snap. Allen's temper reared most notably in a 1938 game in Boston. Allen, infuriated when umpires ordered him to remove his frayed undershirt, stalked to the clubhouse, refusing to play. A $250 fine followed, but Allen never paid it. Instead, the downtown Higbee's department store bought the now-famous shirt as a window display. The money went to pay Allen's fine, infuriating manager Oscar Vitt.

While the Indians of the 1930s languished, hope shimmered on the horizon as a country and a sport prepared to meet the coming decade.

Municipal Stadium was more than a baseball field. The lakefront arena hosted all sorts of events, including minicar races; high school football games; religious gatherings; and civic meetings, such as the Shriners' 57th annual session held July 14-16, 1931.

With his steely blue eyes staring down hitters, Wes Ferrell pitched a no-hitter against the St. Louis Browns on April 29, 1931. For good measure, he helped his own cause with a homer and four RBI. Ferrell's brother, Rick, played for the St. Louis squad that day.

Scoring like a couple of football teams, the Indians and the St. Louis Browns opened the 1925 season with a bang. Cleveland blew a 7-1 lead only to score 12 runs in the eighth inning, thanks to five St. Louis errors. The Indians won 21-14.

34

Although Indians fans mired in mediocre baseball turned out the lights on many seasons, they could still go to sleep dreaming about hitting like Earl Averill when the room went dark.

Mel Harder was the Indians' starting pitcher for Municipal Stadium's first official baseball game, which was played on July 31, 1932. Harder was also on the field for ceremonies when the Indians left the Lakefront and opened Jacobs Field in 1994. He signed this ball that day.

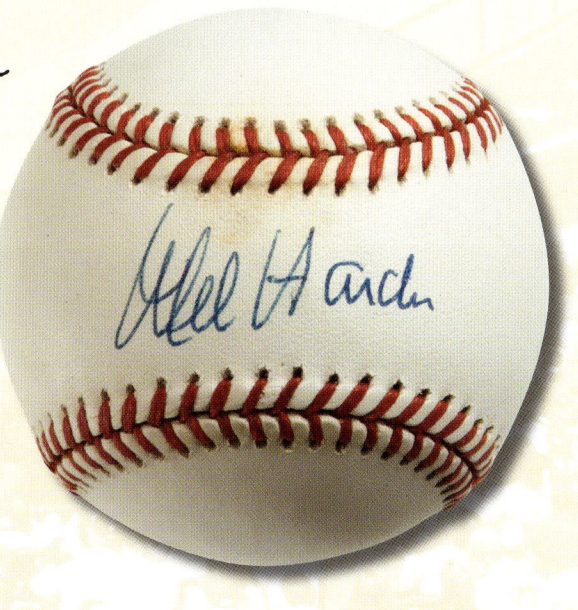

Third baseman Odell "Bad News" Hale spearheaded one uncanny triple play. During a game on September 7, 1935, a smash tore through his glove, hit his head, and caromed straight to shortstop Bill Knickerbocker. The ball was tossed to second and then to first for a triple play.

Lakefront Property

Alva Bradley and his millionaire partners didn't just buy the Indians and League Park. They bought a promise of a grand lakefront stadium to house their team. Former team president Ernest Barnard, who guided the franchise after the death of owner Jim Dunn, saw the prospect of a stadium as a lure to new owners who might be concerned with aging League Park's limited seating and its remote, cramped neighborhood location.

Less than a year after Bradley's group bought the Indians, Cleveland voters passed a $2.5 million bond issue to fund the project that would become Cleveland Municipal Stadium. Bradley believed the lakefront stadium would bring thousands of people closer to downtown and, as an added bonus, to businesses in which he and his partners had a financial interest.

The stadium opened on July 1, 1931, but Indians owners and the city haggled over lease terms. The Indians didn't take the field for the first time until they played the Philadelphia Athletics on July 31, 1932 in front of 80,000 fans—a crowd nearly three times the size of any previous Indians home audience.

Ohio Governor George White tossed the ceremonial first pitch to Cleveland Mayor Ray Miller. A's owner/manager Connie Mack took the microphone and thanked the city for providing "the Indians and all of baseball with such a magnificent structure."

Starting pitcher Mel Harder believed he was supposed to throw a second ceremonial

A view from the center field bleachers on July 25, 1932, six days before the first Indians game, captures the immense playing field that became Municipal Stadium's trademark. This camera angle also depicts the view from the end zone of a football field soon to host the Cleveland Rams and Cleveland Browns.

Compared to the intimacy of League Park, Municipal Stadium put fans out of arm's or ear's reach of the action. But when it was filled with more than 70,000 people, no stadium in baseball could compare.

All-Star Turnout

An All-Star Game crowd of 69,812 fans (a record until 1981) filed into a slightly used Municipal Stadium on July 8, 1935, for the third All-Star Game. It was the first of five midsummer classics Cleveland would host over the years.

Missing the 1935 spectacle was local favorite Earl Averill, who nearly lost his hand to a July 4 fireworks accident. Indians outfielder Joe Vosmik was there and batted leadoff for the AL. Cleveland righthander Mel Harder appeared in his second-straight All-Star Game, and AL manager Mickey Cochrane called on Chief to close out the game. Harder tossed three shutout innings to secure a 4–1 win.

pitch when A's leadoff hitter Max Bishop dug in. Bishop apparently didn't get the memo because he slapped Harder's friendly toss into left field for a single. It was the first Indians mistake in what would come to be known as the "Mistake by the Lake."

With so many fans wearing white shirts in the outfield bleachers, pitchers dominated because the ball was hard to see. Philadelphia's Lefty Grove beat Harder 1–0 in Muny's first game. But fan fashion wasn't the only drain on offense in this immense stadium. The power alleys were a demoralizing 435 feet from the plate. A home run to center would have to travel 470 feet. Home runs, all the rage in baseball, would be scarce in Cleveland.

"This joint will kill your ballclub," Babe Ruth told Indians players.

Fans had their problems with the place, too. Muny's expansive grandstand put fans farther away from the action than they were at League Park, and support beams obscured some views. Clevelanders, feeling the brunt of the Great Depression, rarely filled the ballpark—the average attendance through 1933 was about 6,000. The Indians, citing poor attendance, temporarily cancelled their lease with the city and didn't play at Muny from 1934 to 1936. Bradley later succumbed to pressure from city leaders and in 1937 agreed to play select games at what was being called the "White Elephant."

Municipal Stadium became the Indians' permanent home when new owner Bill Veeck abandoned League Park for good in 1947. Record crowds would come with better teams.

CHAPTER THREE

The Golden Age
1936–1954

OLD-TIMERS LIKE TO talk about better days in Cleveland. They wax poetic about ballplayers living next door, star outfielders needing winter jobs, and thousands cramming the West Third Street Bridge on their way to the game. Those fans didn't go for bobbleheads or dollar dogs but for pennant-race baseball. They debate who was the best of the Big Four. They boast of Feller's heater, the Boudreau Shift, and the hitting exploits of Rosen and Avila. They admire the handy glovework of Keltner. And they marvel at the barriers crossed and crushed by Doby and Easter. They remember Cleveland's Golden Age.

Bob Feller, the Heater from Van Meter, intimidated hitters with a high leg kick that foretold and propelled his searing fastball.

Above: Bob Feller made major-league history when he tossed a no-hitter against the White Sox on Opening Day in 1940 with the help of this ball. *Opposite:* The best trades in baseball are often the ones you don't make. Indians owner Bill Veeck (center) would have agreed. Here, he and Indians player-manager Lou Boudreau (in uniform) whoop it up with coach Bill McKechnie after the Tribe won the 1948 World Series. Veeck wanted to trade fan-favorite Boudreau less than a year earlier.

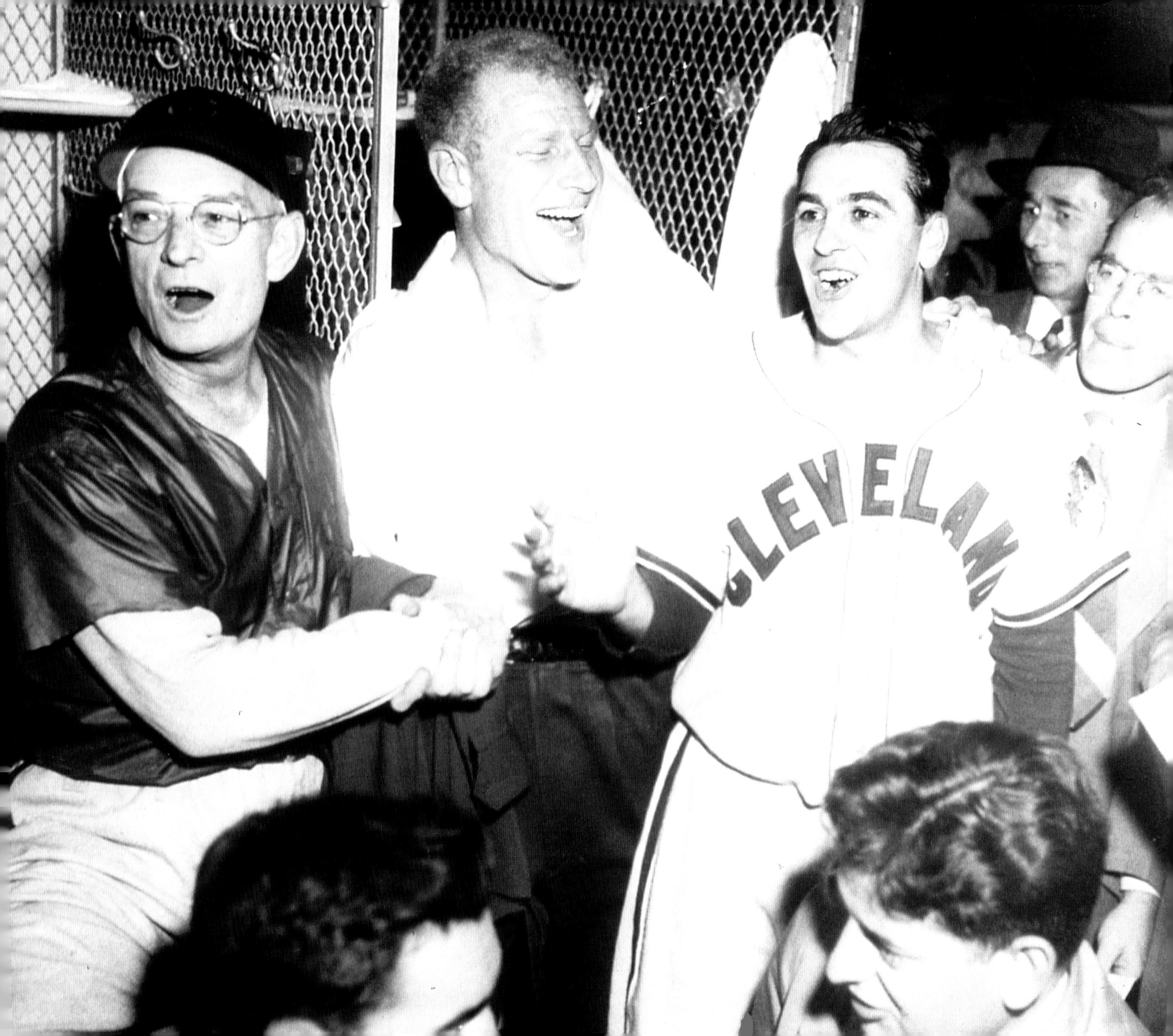
CLEVELAND

Rapid Robert Arrives

Inside a millionaire's Terminal Tower suite surrounded by gruff Indians executives, talent scout Cy Slapnicka rose to his feet, almost choking over his own exuberance. He had uncovered a diamond dandy while working the cornfields of Iowa.

"Gentleman, I've found the greatest young pitcher I ever saw," he began. "This boy I found out in Iowa will be the greatest pitcher the world has ever known."

That pitcher was 17-year-old Robert Feller, who brought hope and moxie to go with a toe-to-the-moon leg kick that propelled a blazing fastball. The kid debuted in an exhibition game on July 6, 1936, against the St. Louis Cardinals at League Park. Rapid Robert struck out eight members of the Gashouse Gang in three innings of work. Only 9,000 fans witnessed the feat, but they saw the birth of a legend.

With the team's pennant hopes fading, owner Alva Bradley showcased Feller. He struck out 15 St. Louis Browns in his first big-league start. Three weeks later, Feller fanned 17 Philadelphia Athletics, setting a new AL single-game strikeout record and tying the major-league single-game record. He finished his rookie year with a 5–3 record—and then went home to finish high school.

Feller's blazing fastball was easy to credit for his success, but it wasn't the only weapon in his arsenal. He also had a wicked curve. Even the great Yankee Clipper admired the bender.

"[His curveball] came in so fast and broke so sharply that it was almost as though Feller was wrenching the bat out of your hand and shoving it down your throat," Joe DiMaggio recalled.

Feller won 24 games in 1939, 27 in 1940, and 25 in 1941. He also struck out 246, 261, and 260 batters in those years, respectively. With all that success, commercial endorsements and adoration followed his every step.

But he might have been more admired for *not* playing baseball from 1942 through most of the 1945 season. Two days after the Japanese attack on Pearl Harbor, Feller walked to a Navy recruitment office and enlisted.

It's a colossal understatement to say Rapid Robert was in the prime of his career when he joined the service. In his first full season after spending 44 months in the Navy, he won a league-high 26 games and struck out a record 348 batters. Estimates are

While most high school seniors look for themselves in their yearbooks, 18-year-old Bob Feller found himself on Time. The Tribe's pitching phenom graced the magazine's April 19, 1937, cover as he prepared for his second year of major-league baseball.

Technology in Feller's time never caught up with Rapid Robert's fastball. In 1946 at the Army's Aberdeen Proving Grounds, this device made of photoelectric cells measured Feller's pitch at an estimated 98 mph. A race against a motorcycle delivered the same results. In later years, Feller said he easily would have topped 105 mph on a modern radar gun.

Terminal Velocity

Frankie Pytlak caught Indians pitchers for nine seasons, and backstop Hank Helf worked seven games over two summers. Each saw a fastball or two in their day, but nothing compares to the 138-mph heaters they snared on August 20, 1938.

To promote Cleveland's 52-story Terminal Tower, Pytlak and Helf put on their mitts and caught balls that were dropped from the top floor in front of more than 10,000 curious people in Public Square. Helf nabbed his ball one-handed.

"Nothing to it," Helf boasted. "I just kept my eye on the ball all the way down."

Pytlak corralled his toss using both hands.

"It stung more than Bob Feller's fast one," he told reporters.

Terminal Tower

---

that he lost about 100 wins and 1,000 strikeouts to his military service.

Although the postseason proved troubling for Feller (he didn't win a World Series game in either 1948 or 1954), he retired as Cleveland's all-time greatest pitcher, with 266 wins and 2,581 strikeouts. He tossed three no-hitters, including an Opening Day gem in 1940, and 12 one-hitters.

Looking back on his start as a fireballing teenager, Feller told a reporter: "I didn't know much. I just reared back and let them go. Where the ball went was up to heaven. Sometimes I threw the ball clear up in the stands."

Above: There wasn't much Bob Feller couldn't do with a baseball in his hand. His only regret in a Hall of Fame career was not winning a World Series game. He went 0–2 in the 1948 classic and didn't appear in the 1954 Series. *Right:* Bob Feller is ubiquitous in retirement. Whether it's spring training, Opening Day, or he's simply somewhere sipping coffee, fans can always count on Rapid Robert for some baseball talk and an autograph.

There *Is* Crying in Baseball

Owner Alva Bradley couldn't believe his ears. Key members of the 1940 Indians, in the midst of the team's finest season since 1926, begged him to fire manager Oscar "Ossie" Vitt, a tyrannical leader known for blasting players in the newspapers. Bradley was in his office when veteran pitcher Mel Harder and a dozen other players came knocking.

"If we could get rid of him, we can win," Harder implored.

Harder's plea was interrupted by a phone call from slugging first baseman Hal Trosky, who added his support for firing Vitt. Bradley ended the meeting with a harsh warning: If word of this coup attempt got out, the Indians would be a major-league joke.

It did, and they were.

Word hit the papers in mid-June. Soon fans and opponents were calling the team the Cleveland Crybabies. Somehow, despite all the baby talk, the Indians found themselves in first place heading into a late-September series in Detroit. The taunting reached a fevered pitch in Motown, where 5,000 fans showered the Indians with heckles, eggs, and vegetables as soon as they exited their train. Baby bottle nipples dangled above the Cleveland dugout at Briggs Stadium when the teams played.

The Indians dropped two of three games and fell from first after the Tiger series. They ended up in second, one game behind Detroit. The Crybabies got their wish on October 28 when Bradley fired Vitt.

The Clipper Gets Clipped

Ken Keltner made seven AL All-Star Teams as a power-hitting third baseman with the Indians, but he got national attention for what his glove did to Joe DiMaggio's hitting streak on July 17, 1941.

In the series opener at League Park, the Yankee Clipper banged three hits, pushing his streak to 56 games. The next night, the game moved to Municipal Stadium. With southpaw Al Smith pitching, Keltner played deep at third, hugging the foul line. Two potential DiMaggio doubles died in Keltner's leather as the third-bagger backhanded the smashes. The streak was over.

Joe DiMaggio playfully got revenge on Ken Keltner during an old-timers game in 1966.

Perhaps no team in baseball endured the torment that shadowed the 1940 Indians after players concocted a midseason coup attempt on manager Oscar Vitt. In Detroit, fans showered the field with trash and taunted the Tribe with baby bottles and nipples.

Country Came First

Bob Feller led the way with urgency, volunteering for the Navy three days after the Day of Infamy. Other Indians, including Ken Keltner; Hank Edwards; Jim Bagby, Jr.; Gene Woodling; and Bob Lemon, would follow. Larry Doby, then a Negro Leagues star, would serve, too.

America was at war in 1941, and all hands were on deck. More than 500 big-leaguers and 5,000 minor-leaguers would serve during World War II.

Feller was a 22-year-old star when he stunned teammates and fans with his enlistment on December 10, 1941. He refused deferments and didn't hide during his four years in the service. Feller served in the Navy as a chief petty officer and gun captain, winning eight battle stars. He estimates he crossed the equator more than two dozen times aboard the USS *Alabama* as his crew pursued the Japanese off the South Pacific islands.

The war made Lemon a Hall of Famer. He was an Indians third baseman and outfielder in 1941 before joining the Navy; he learned to pitch while playing for Navy teams. That training proved fruitful because he joined the Indians pitching staff in 1946 and went on to win 207 games.

Keltner's string of five straight All-Star Games ended when he left in 1945 for a Navy stint in Hawaii. He returned the next year and resumed his stellar work at third base. Doby left the Negro Leagues and joined the Navy in 1944. He was stationed on the same island as major-leaguers Mickey Vernon and Billy Goodman, and they played ball together. Both told Doby he had the ability to make it in the show—but all these men had more pressing issues at hand.

Nick Mueller, president of the World War II museum, summed it up best: "They risked their big-league careers for a cause that was greater than glory on the diamond."

Bob Feller shelved his fastball and enlisted with the U.S. Naval Reserve just three days after Japan bombed Pearl Harbor. The 22-year-old superstar was sworn in by Lt. Comm. Gene Tunney to begin a four-year stretch during World War II.

MORE THAN 50 YEARS AFTER PITCHING HIS LAST GAME IN CLEVELAND, BOB FELLER REMAINS REVERED BY TRIBE FAITHFUL. FELLER'S BOBBLEHEAD SYMBOLIZES HIS POPULARITY AS THE INDIANS' LIVING LEGEND.

INDIANS FANS TRAVELING DOWNTOWN NEEDED ONLY TO LOOK FOR THE INDIANS FLAG ATOP THE TERMINAL TOWER TO KNOW IT WAS GAME DAY. TEAM PROGRAMS REMINDED THE FAITHFUL TO LOOK UP.

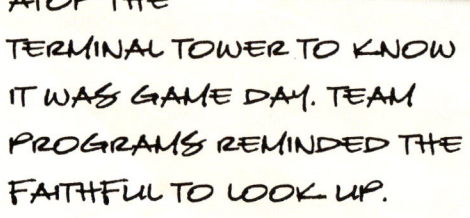

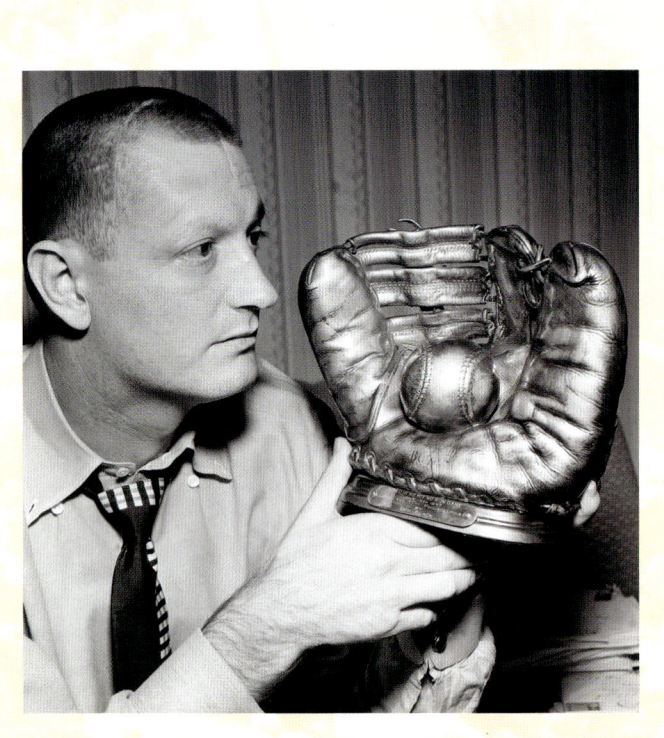

DON BLACK BATTLED ALCOHOL, HEALTH PROBLEMS, AND AL BATTERS FOR THE INDIANS, TOSSING A NO-HITTER IN 1947. HIS WIFE HAD HIS GLOVE FROM THE NO-HITTER BRONZED FOR POSTERITY.

THE FIRST PITCH OF THE 1948 WORLD SERIES WAS DELIVERED BY THE BRAVES' JOHNNY SAIN TO INDIANS LEADOFF MAN DALE MITCHELL, WHO EVENTUALLY FLEW OUT TO CENTER FIELD.

44

BOB FELLER WAS SO FAMOUS HE CREATED HIS OWN COMPANY AND REGISTERED HIS NAME WITH THE U.S. PATENT OFFICE FOR SLOGANS SUCH AS "GOOD FELLER" AND "HI-FELLER."

HE WASN'T THE FLEETEST AFOOT, BUT LOU BOUDREAU'S HANDS WERE SURE. PLUS, HE WAS POPULAR, MAKING HIM A NATURAL TO PEN A BOOK ABOUT PLAYING THE INFIELD.

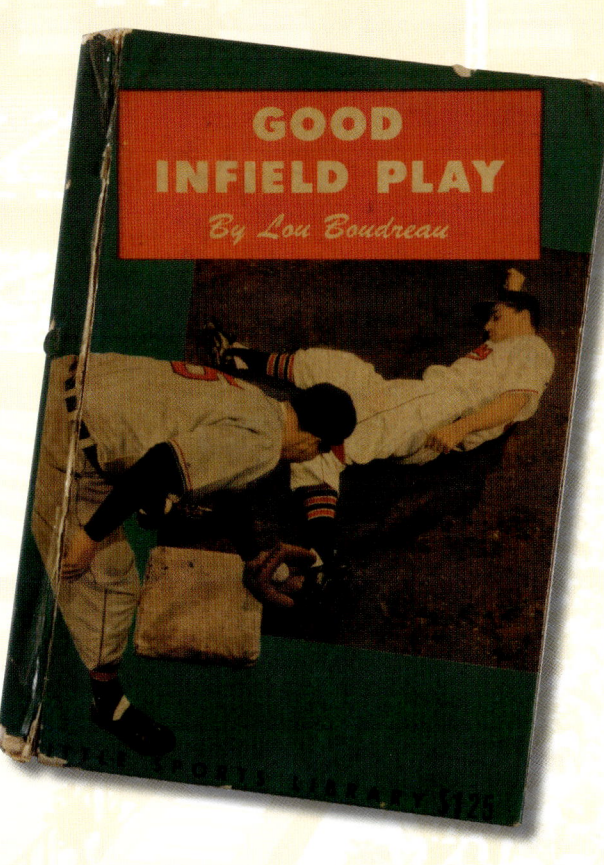

MORE THAN 200,000 PEOPLE WELCOMED HOME THE INDIANS AFTER THE 1948 SERIES IN A PARADE LED BY THE WAVES OF LOU BOUDREAU AND BILL VEECK. CONVERTIBLES ESCORTED THE CITY HEROES DOWN EUCLID AVENUE.

CLEVELAND NATIVE BOB HOPE WASN'T JOKING AS HE CHEERED ON HIS INDIANS. HE PUT HIS MONEY WHERE HIS HEART WAS: HE BECAME AN INDIANS STOCKHOLDER UNDER BILL VEECK.

Bill Veeck's Tribal Revival

Bill Veeck, Jr., rolled into Cleveland as baseball's version of P. T. Barnum. He was a showman wrapped in acumen and guile tucked not so neatly beneath his scouring pad strawberry-blond hair, open collar, and plastic-framed glasses.

Cleveland fans, anxious for a title after 26 seasons of waiting 'til next year, braced themselves for the unpredictable Veeck, who had built a carnival-act reputation as owner of the minor-league Milwaukee Brewers. The Brewers won three minor-league titles, and attendance soared as Veeck threw just about every marketing trick against the wall. He introduced Milwaukee fans to on-field circus acts, a movable outfield fence, and door prizes that included blocks of ice and live lobsters.

In 1946, the 32-year-old Veeck bought the Indians with borrowed money and a saddle of investors, including Cleveland native Bob Hope. Stuffy-shirted baseball experts were surprised to find that his bag of sparkling fireworks, strolling grandstand musicians, livestock prizes for fans, and nylons for women on Ladies Day played well in the bigs. Veeck also hired pitcher-turned-entertainer Max Patkin, who would later become known as the "Clown Prince of Baseball" to "coach" at first base.

"Bill's philosophy was even the best team in history lost games," said Marsh Samuel, Veeck's childhood friend and the Indians' public relations chief in 1947. "He wanted to give fans something more on the days when the team didn't win."

Veeck was pure Cleveland. As a beer-swigging cigarette smoker, he felt at home

From animal acts to lingerie, Bill Veeck had a million ways to draw crowds. In his 1962 autobiography, Veeck As In Wreck, he reveals the brains behind his seat-filling circus act that came to Cleveland in 1947.

Bill Veeck might have lost a leg in World War II, but he gained a clown in Max Patkin. The two met during the war, where Patkin was a soldier and a part-time goofball pitcher. Veeck brought the Clown Prince to Cleveland as a "coach" and entertainer.

Cleveland Municipal Stadium to see Paige's debut. But Paige's 6–1 season was a key component to Cleveland's second World Series title. So was Doby's bat.

Veeck's diamond cabaret didn't last long, but he knew how to make an exit. When his 1949 team was mathematically eliminated from pennant contention, he orchestrated a funeral promotion in which the Indians buried the 1948 pennant in the stadium outfield. Before the 1950 season, Veeck sold his interest in the Indians, in part to satisfy a messy divorce settlement. The carnival left town, but Cleveland had won the big prize.

Ashes to ashes, World Series to third place. Bill Veeck, ever the showman, couldn't resist mocking his team's misfortune following the 1948 championship. To ease the pain of failing to repeat, Veeck held a September funeral in 1949 and buried the 1948 Series pennant.

sitting with fans in the bleachers or in a neighborhood tavern talking baseball and apologizing for trying to trade Lou Boudreau. Indians fans felt the connection, too; more than 1 million people clicked the turnstiles in 1947. That was nearly double 1946's attendance, and it was the first time the Indians had ever drawn seven figures.

But the showman was a shrewd baseball man who traded for key players such as Joe Gordon and Early Wynn. He also integrated the American League by signing Negro Leagues star Larry Doby in 1947. Legendary Negro Leagues pitcher Satchel Paige would join the club midway through the 1948 season. Some thought that signing was just a publicity stunt. Indeed, 65,000 showed up at

Good Old Joe Earley Night

Bill Veeck knew a good promotion when he heard one, and Joe Earley provided the fodder in September 1948. In response to all the ballpark events that honored players, the night watchman wrote a letter to the editor suggesting Veeck honor long-suffering, cash-strapped fans, like himself. Veeck complied, always eager to please his customers.

"Good Old Joe Earley Night" drew 60,000 fans, many of whom shared in the bounty. Veeck flew in orchids from Hawaii for female fans. Other fans got live rabbits or ladders.

Before the night was over, Veeck turned the stadium into an early version of *Let's Make a Deal*. He lavished gag gifts, such as an outhouse and a beat-up Model T, on Earley before rolling out humdingers that included a new convertible, kitchen appliances, and $5,400.

Joe Earley and his wife

Doby Follows Jackie, Leads AL

Reporters gathered around owner Bill Veeck on July 3, 1947, for news of a key acquisition. "We've signed a new ballplayer named Larry Doby," Veeck announced. His next words startled the pale-faced press.

"He's a Negro."

Veeck was determined to break the AL color line, but he had to have the right player to do so. He assigned a scout to follow 22-year-old Doby, a second baseman with the Newark Eagles of the Negro National League, for weeks to ensure the groundbreaking move would succeed. This wasn't one of Veeck's stunts. His new player's job was to trailblaze the AL and take the same arduous road Jackie Robinson had set out on 11 weeks earlier with the Brooklyn Dodgers.

Like Robinson had been, Doby was restrained by rules no white player would tolerate. If balls were called strikes, Doby would have to remain silent. If taunted, he must turn his cheek. If spat on after a close play at second, he must walk away.

Restraint was the only way the experiment would work.

"I was on trial," Doby would later say.

Although some Indians players welcomed their new mate, others refused to even shake Doby's hand. Veeck said he received 20,000 letters, most brimming with hatred and threats, over the signing.

Far left: Larry Doby was Bill Veeck's choice to break the American League color barrier in 1947. The move paid dividends as Doby had a Hall of Fame career, making seven All-Star Teams while knocking in more than 100 runs for Cleveland four times and twice leading the AL in home runs. *Left:* While Jackie Robinson paved the way through National League parks after first playing in the Dodger farm system, Larry Doby went straight from the Negro Leagues to the American League, visiting parks and cities that had never seen an African American man in a major-league uniform.

But there wasn't much time to think about all that. Unlike Robinson, Doby didn't play minor-league ball to acclimate himself to white teammates and fans—he went straight to the majors. On July 5, Doby stepped into the batter's box at Chicago's Comiskey Park and struck out while integrating the AL.

Doby rode the bench most of the rest of the 1947 season, but the dugout didn't shield him from the ridicule launched by racist fans from St. Louis to Boston. He hit just .156 in 32 at-bats, most of which were pinch-hit appearances.

Doby would emerge in 1948 after switching positions and working his way into the lineup as the Indians' starting center fielder. He hit .301 with 14 homers while honing his outfield skills for the eventual champions. He became the first black player to hit a round-tripper in a World Series game when he did so with a 410-foot blast in Game 4.

Teammate Al Rosen recalled the bumpy road Doby took. In a game against Detroit, pitcher Dizzy Trout dusted him four times.

"But Larry just got up, brushed himself off, and walked to first base," Rosen told sportswriter Russell Schneider. "I've always admired him."

In his 13-year career, Doby would make seven All-Star Games and twice lead the AL in home runs. His 215 homers as an Indian rank sixth all-time. Doby later coached with the Indians and managed the Chicago White Sox, becoming the second African American to lead a club. The Indians retired Doby's No. 14 when he was inducted into baseball's Hall of Fame in 1998.

Larry Doby, pictured here with Lou Boudreau, made his American League debut at Comiskey Park in Chicago three hours after signing his contract on July 5, 1947. Doby struck out as a pinch hitter, but he proved his signing was no Bill Veeck publicity stunt.

The Buckeyes Have It

Cleveland had a World Series winner in 1945, but the championship was largely ignored and has nearly been forgotten.

The Cleveland Buckeyes were one of the best squads in the Negro Leagues during the 1940s, although they drew modest crowds to League Park and Cleveland Municipal Stadium. Led by Sam Jethroe, Willie Grace, and Quincy Trouppe, the team won the Negro American League title in 1945 and 1947.

The 1945 Negro League World Series pitted the Buckeyes against the vaunted Homestead Grays, a legendary team that boasted stars like "Cool Papa" Bell, Josh Gibson, and Buck Leonard. The Buckeyes swept the Grays in four games, but the championship was back-page news in Cleveland.

The Boy Wonder

It was one of those it's-so-crazy-it-just-might-work ideas: Owner Alva Bradley decided that Lou Boudreau, all of 24 years old, would manage the Indians in 1942. In three seasons, Boudreau had become one of the league's finest shortstops—a field general with talent. His good looks and skills made him popular among Indians fans, and Little Leaguers emulated his unique hook-shape batting stance.

Boudreau entered his first spring training as manager without his best power hitter and his stalwart pitcher. Hal Trosky's migraines had forced him into retirement, while Pearl Harbor spurred Bob Feller to join the Navy. That spring, Boudreau proved naive, as well, asking Cleveland sportswriters to show him their stories before they submitted them to their editors. He feared criticism would harm his team. When the laughter stopped, the writers said no.

Boudreau had the Indians contending in 1942, before fortunes faded and the team finished fourth, 28 games out. There was a fear that managing would hurt Boudreau's play, but he was an All-Star from 1942 to 1945. In fact, he led the AL in 1944 with a .327 average.

Shabby ankles made Boudreau ineligible for World War II and probably saved his managerial career. His teams, loaded with has-beens and have-nots, finished no higher than third. But over the years, he grew as a strategist, creating the fabled "Boudreau Shift," in which he stationed most of his players to the right side of the diamond to defend the pull-hitting of left-handed star Ted Williams (Boudreau's strategy was also called the "Williams Shift").

New owner Bill Veeck almost traded Boudreau in 1947. Only public outrage saved the Boy Manager's job. The outcry was rewarded the following autumn.

Fan-favorite shortstop Lou Boudreau talked Indians owner Alva Bradley into making him player-manager in 1942 at the tender age of 24. Here he talks with veteran Washington manager Bucky Harris. In his first six seasons, Boudreau's teams finished no higher than third, but things changed in 1948.

Indian Summer, 1948

An unexpected citywide buzz built up soon after the first pitch of 1948. The Indians won their first six games. By June, they were 31–13 and in first place.

"In spring training, I didn't think about us being a contender," said first baseman Eddie Robinson. "But soon after the season started, my roommate, Joe Gordon, said, 'You know, I think we can win this thing.' That's the first I thought of winning the pennant."

But the Indians weren't the only ones who thought they had a chance. The Athletics, Yankees, and Red Sox also battled for the AL flag all summer. The Tribe kept pace with key acquisitions, a prime farm system, and veterans having career years. Crowds topped 80,000 on occasion; a record 2.6 million visited the park in all.

Not everyone believed. Al Simmons, an A's coach, told reporters: "Don't worry about the Indians. They'll choke up. They always do."

Indeed, panic came in September. Boudreau banned reporters from the clubhouse, stadium groundskeepers helped steal signs with a telescope, and fans booed Bob Feller. Then it clicked. With 14 wins in 16 games, Cleveland reclaimed first place with a week to go. On the final day, the Indians fell to Detroit while the Red Sox beat the Yankees, setting up a one-game playoff with Boston, the first playoff in AL history.

Indians left-hander Gene Bearden dominated Red Sox bats. Lou Boudreau homered twice, and Ken Keltner tagged a three-run shot as the Tribe won 8–3. Baseball's biggest stage awaited.

Lou Boudreau had his choice of future Hall of Fame hurlers for a one-game playoff against Boston, but it was rookie southpaw Gene Bearden who was carried off the field after pitching the Indians into the 1948 World Series.

Cleveland's Unlikely Star

Gene Bearden was lucky to be alive, let alone a Cleveland hero. Aboard the USS *Helena* during World War II, more than 200 Navy men died when the ship was sunk. Bearden emerged injured and was told he'd never pitch again.

Instead, he pitched brilliantly for one uncanny season.

The left-handed knuckleballer, a throw-in from a trade with the Yankees, went 20–7 for the Indians in 1948. On a day's rest, he beat Boston in a one-game pennant playoff, propelling the Indians to the World Series.

Bill Veeck called Bearden "the biggest surprise I've ever had in baseball."

But AL hitters quickly learned to lay off Bearden's knuckleballs. He won only 25 games the rest of his career while playing with four other teams.

Tribe on Top

The summer of 1948 was a great time to be in Cleveland. War was a memory, jobs were plentiful, the football Browns and hockey Barons were champions, and the Indians provided Clevelanders a summer-long drama as inviting as it was compelling.

Housewives, grandmothers, and even little kids could rattle off the names of the Indians, from Lou Boudreau to Sam Zoldak. From Opening Day in April right through to the World Series in October, Municipal Stadium or near the living room radio was the place to be for baseball. People cared about this team. Bill Veeck made it fun.

"It was both the climax of one era in the history of baseball, and the beginning of another," wrote David Kaiser in his book *Epic Season, The 1948 American League Pennant Race*. "And even those who lived through it often forget exactly how incredible it was."

The Indians weren't the most talented team nor were they the most feared. In fact, they were a 20–1 long shot to win the AL pennant. They never played that way.

Huge crowds crammed Municipal Stadium for a knuckle-gnawing pennant race that, for once, actually went Cleveland's way. Once they had their ticket punched to the Series, there was no way this team was going to lose. Not this year, not this team. The Boston Braves were a mere stepping-stone to a championship, but they weren't to be taken lightly. The Braves boasted a pitching staff of humble lore: "Spahn and Sain and pray for rain," as the saying went. Tommy Holmes topped an order that led the NL in batting average.

Johnny Sain faced off against Bob Feller in Game 1 in Boston. It proved a pitcher's duel, with Feller throwing five no-hit innings before being touched for a run in the eighth. The run came after an umpire blew a call at second base on a perfectly executed pickoff move by Feller and Boudreau. The Braves

Steve Gromek pitched a complete-game 2–1 victory in Game 4, the same contest in which Larry Doby became the first African American to hit a home run in a World Series game. The photograph of them embracing after the game, however, carried more impact than their performances on the field that day.

Indians pitchers Bob Lemon (*left*) and Gene Bearden (*center*) celebrate with catcher Jim Hegan, who many Tribe fans consider the team's best defensive backstop ever. Over a 17-year career, Hegan made five All-Star appearances and guided some of baseball's best pitchers.

Left: Some of the 86,288 Indians fans attending Game 5 of the 1948 World Series make their way over a bridge along West Third Street, heading toward parking lots, bus lines, and trains. Tribe fans would set season and World Series attendance records at Municipal Stadium that year. *Below:* Managers Lou Boudreau and the Boston Braves' Billy Southworth matched wits and photos in the 1948 World Series. As an outfielder, Southworth made his big-league debut with Cleveland in 1913. Boudreau would end his playing career in Boston with the Red Sox.

won 1–0. Two future Hall of Famers went head to head in Game 2. In the end, Bob Lemon bested Warren Spahn 4–1 as Boudreau and Larry Doby led the Indian attack.

Finally, it was off to Cleveland. Ticket snafus and rain softened attendance—*only* 70,306 saw Gene Bearden continue his Cinderella season with a five-hit shutout, as the Indians won 2–0. After three games, Tribe pitchers had given up two runs. Game 4 brought out 81,897 as Steve Gromek outpitched Sain, and the Indians took a 3–1 lead in the Series.

Prospects of a World Series victory before frenzied Cleveland fans sent electricity through the air. And why not? Feller was pitching in Game 5, and the Braves bats were snoozing. A crowd of 86,288, a World Series record until 1959, was poised to light up Euclid Avenue. But the Braves lit up Feller instead. Boston's Bob Elliott belted a three-run homer in the first inning and a solo shot in the third as the Braves swiped Game 5 11–5 and sent the Series back to Beantown.

In Game 6, Lemon kept the Braves in check, Boudreau and Joe Gordon supplied the offense, and Bearden closed the door in the ninth for the 4–3 Series-winning Cleveland victory. Thousands greeted the team's train from Boston at Union Station underneath Terminal Tower. Later, more than 200,000 fans lined downtown streets cheering their well-dressed heroes who rode in convertibles. Cleveland could get used to this, but the baseball gods had something else in mind.

CHARLIE LUPICA MISSED DINNER, BUT HIS WIFE DIDN'T WORRY. LUPICA SPENT 117 DAYS ATOP A MAKESHIFT FLAGPOLE IN 1949, REFUSING TO SURRENDER UNTIL THE INDIANS OFFICIALLY LOST THE PENNANT.

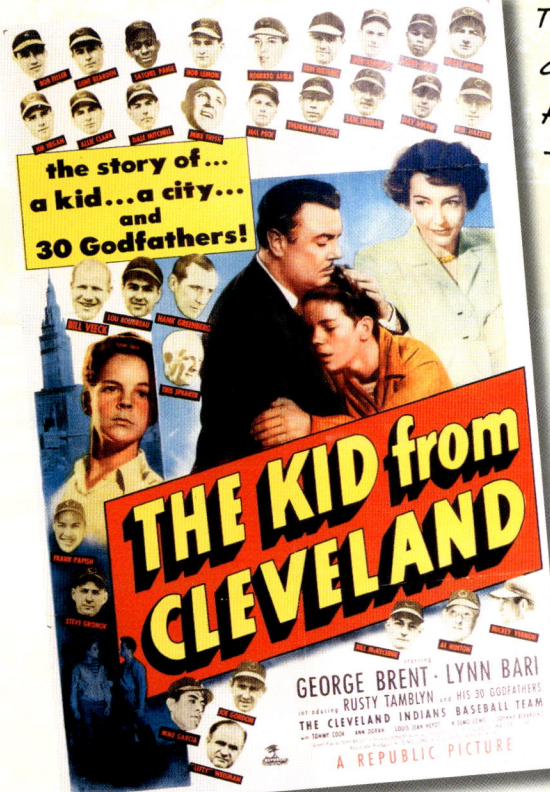

THE KID FROM CLEVELAND, A MOVIE ABOUT A TROUBLED TEENAGER WHO WAS HELPED BY A BUNCH OF INDIANS, OFFERED BREATHTAKING VIEWS OF CLEVELAND. THE MOVIE ITSELF, WHICH FEATURED REAL CLEVELAND INDIANS, WAS NOT SO BREATHTAKING.

WHEN RONALD REAGAN (RIGHT) NEEDED PITCHING TIPS IN ORDER TO PORTRAY GROVER CLEVELAND ALEXANDER IN THE 1952 MOVIE THE WINNING TEAM, HE TURNED TO INDIANS STALWART BOB LEMON.

BOB FELLER WAS NEARING THE END OF HIS STORIED PITCHING CAREER WHEN HE NOTCHED HIS 250TH WIN IN 1954. FELLER WOULD WIN 13 THAT YEAR.

INFIELDER JOHNNY BERARDINO WASN'T A DOCTOR, HE JUST EVENTUALLY PLAYED ONE (STEVE HARDY) ON TV'S GENERAL HOSPITAL. BILL VEECK SAW HIS POTENTIAL AND JUST FOR FUN HAD THE HANDSOME ACTOR'S FACE INSURED.

IT COST JUST $7 FOR A GOOD LOWER-DECK SEAT TO SEE THE WORLD SERIES AT MUNICIPAL STADIUM.

BOB LEMON WON 20 GAMES IN SEVEN DIFFERENT SEASONS FOR THE INDIANS AFTER BEING CONVERTED FROM THIRD BASE. HIS NO. 21 IS RETIRED BY THE TRIBE.

The One and Only Satchel Paige

Bill Veeck personally scouted a hotshot rookie to help manager Lou Boudreau with the 1948 pennant drive. In a covert audition at Municipal Stadium, Boudreau caught some pitches from and took some cuts against the lanky right-hander.

"I'll take him," Boudreau said.

Leroy "Satchel" Paige, easily the most famous star of the Negro Leagues, had finally arrived in the majors. No one knew exactly how old he was. Paige claimed he was 42, but others put his age at 48.

His delivery was herky-jerky, with some hesitation moves dropped in. His fastball, no one could hit. His persona, no one could emulate. At his one-liners, no one could keep a straight face. He had names for his pitches, such as droopers and loopers. He also tossed a "be-ball," so named because "it be where I want it to be," Satch would say.

The national media called Paige's signing a publicity stunt pulled by carnival barker Veeck. Paige was a gate attraction; he'd been packing them in all over the Western Hemisphere since the 1920s. But Satch would do a lot more than sell tickets. He went 6–1 down the stretch while appearing in 21 games. No one knows what could have been had Paige been able to debut 20 years earlier.

"They said I was the greatest pitcher they ever saw," he said. "I couldn't understand why they couldn't give me no justice."

Legendary pitcher Satchel Paige came to Cleveland in 1948, bringing with him a caseload of quotes and quips, including: "Just take the ball and throw it where you want to. Throw strikes. Home plate don't move."

Better Late Than Never

In his heyday, they called Luke Easter the "Black Babe Ruth." Cleveland fans saw why on June 23, 1950, when he hit a home run to a yellow upper-deck seat in Municipal Stadium's Section 4. The 477-foot blast was the longest ever hit there.

Easter starred for the Homestead Grays of the Negro National League before signing with the Indians in 1949 at the twilight of his career. Easter said he was 34, but speculation held that he was older. From 1950 to 1954, Easter hit 93 home runs as the Tribe's first baseman before creaky knees ended his career. In 1979, the 63-year-old Easter, working as a Cleveland union steward, was killed during a robbery.

The Second-Place Skipper

Sorry, Leo Durocher, nice guys don't always finish last. Sometimes, they just finish second.

As a major-league manager for 17 seasons, Al Lopez's teams were AL runners-up 10 times. Still, he's a Hall of Famer, one of the most successful managers of all time. During his six seasons managing the Indians (1951–1956), "El Señor" claimed just one pennant. In five other summers, his clubs finished second to the New York Yankee dynasty.

"He was the consummate gentleman, and you knew he was always in your corner," said former Indians infielder Al Rosen.

Lopez came to Cleveland in 1946 at the end of a career that saw him set the record for most games by a catcher (1,918). Owner Bill Veeck saw Lopez as Lou Boudreau's immediate successor as manager, but when fans became outraged at the possible trade of player-manager Boudreau, Lopez took a minor-league managing job and waited.

When Lopez finally took over, the Indians won at least 92 games in each of his first three seasons, but they still finished behind the Yankees. It took a historic 111-win season in 1954 to displace the Bronx Bombers. Afterward, Lopez's Indians were bridesmaids for two more seasons.

Lopez went on to manage the Chicago White Sox, where his team won the pennant in 1959, beating out the second-place Indians. Five of his Chicago teams finished second, but Lopez never had a losing full season in his managerial career.

Close, But No Crown

Casey Stengel said it, so it must be true.

"That feller's a real competitor, you bet your sweet curse life," the Yankee manager quipped.

That competitor was Indians third baseman Al Rosen, who chased the Triple Crown in 1953. Assured the home run and RBI titles, Rosen trailed Washington's Mickey Vernon in the batting race by .003 points heading into the final game.

Rosen went 3-for-5, grounding out on a contested umpire's call at first in his last at-bat. Vernon, who went 2-for-4, couldn't risk another try, so his teammates helped him by running into outs. Vernon hit .337. Rosen hit .336 with 43 home runs and 145 RBI and was named MVP—it wasn't the Triple Crown, but it was still a nice consolation prize.

Al Lopez hammed it up for photographers before the 1954 World Series, but no manager was more highly regarded for his ability to handle a pitching staff. "This man knows the game—inside and out," Casey Stengel once said of Lopez.

The Evolution of Chief Wahoo

It's arguably one of the most recognizable logos in all of sports. Without question, it's the most controversial.

Chief Wahoo, the grinning, big-toothed, red-faced logo of the Indians, appears today on all kinds of team paraphernalia. Indians gear is a top-seller, despite Cleveland being a small-market city. In the glory days of the 1990s, the Indians ranked behind only the Yankees in total sales. At the same time, an increasing number of critics view the logo as stereotypical and racist. Chief Wahoo has been deemphasized in recent years, but he remains the face of the Indians marketing department. Team officials defend the drawing, saying it is not intended to demean.

Chief Wahoo dates back to the late 1920s. At first, the logo was a profile of a distinguished Indian chief. For the 1928 season, Wahoo appeared on the chest of jerseys. Afterward, it was relegated to jersey sleeves and warm-up jackets. The logo only moderately changed over the years.

In 1947, Indians owner Bill Veeck was looking for a snazzier symbol to market his team. Walter Goldbach, a 17-year-old, created the original cartoonish character. With yellow skin, a long nose, sly grin, and a single feather, Chief Wahoo appeared on team jersey sleeves and jackets.

"The last thing on my mind was trying to offend anybody," Goldbach told the Associated Press years later.

In the early 1950s, *Cleveland Plain Dealer* newspaper artist Fred Reinert crafted the red-faced Wahoo familiar today to millions. The newspaper used the drawing daily during the baseball season. The paper printed a smiling Wahoo when the Indians won, and a black-eyed, sad Wahoo reflected a loss. Eventually, the team dropped Goldbach's version and adopted Reinert's drawing, which has adorned the team's caps, jerseys, and jackets over the years.

Depictions of the Indians' mascot have changed over the years, as have feelings about using Native American images to represent sports teams.

Voices of the Tribe

They illustrated with their voices, brushing backyards, living rooms, and cars with portraits of triumphs and miscues. From Jack Graney to Jimmy Dudley, from Bob Neal to Herb Score, the men with the microphone provided a landscape of memories for generations of Indians fans.

Every team, it seemed, had a Southern radio voice telling its story. Cleveland had Dudley, a Virginian with a friend-next-door delivery. He started on WJW-AM radio in 1948, teamed with Graney, a former Indian outfielder, who began broadcasting in 1929.

Dudley would start each game with, "Hello, baseball fans everywhere," and Graney provided insights only a baseball player could. Although untrained as a professional, his delivery was sound.

"His voice dripped with sincerity and crackled with vitality," said Cleveland sportswriter Bob Dolgan.

Dudley would remain a fixture through 1967, paired at times with Neal and Harry Jones. Dudley and Neal didn't like each other, and seldom spoke. At times, Dudley would do the first three and last three innings, ending games with his trademark line, "So long and lots of good luck, ya hear." Neal did the middle three frames.

Score, a phenomenal Indians pitcher until he was injured by a line drive in 1957, was a Cleveland broadcasting icon, first on TV and then as Dudley's radio replacement in 1968. For 30 seasons, Score's low-key voice, despite occasional gaffes, soothed ears.

He had several radio partners, including Joe Tait, who gabbed with Score for seven years at WWWE-AM. Score was cool; Tait was excitable. "It's a beee-u-tiful day for baseball!" Tait would exclaim, no matter the weather.

Score's career covered the team's leanest years, and he saw more losing games than anyone. While teamed with Tom Hamilton, Score called his final contest: Game 7 of the 1997 World Series. The Indians lost in extra innings.

No one has witnessed more losses than Herb Score, who broadcast Tribe games on TV and radio for more than 30 seasons. Score's down-home delivery made long summers easier on Indians fans' ears.

Waaaay back—gone! When Indians fans remember the glory years of the 1990s, it's the booming voice of Tom Hamilton and his signature home run call that comes through loud and clear. Hamilton's enthusiasm is available throughout the year to anyone lucky enough to have scored one of these talking-Tom bobblehead dolls.

The Big Four Fall Short

Indians fans to this day still wonder: How? Why?

The 1954 Indians won 111 games, an American League record at the time. They had the Big Four—possibly the best pitching staff ever assembled; three of those hurlers would end up in the Hall of Fame. Their lineup had power and speed. They hit for average. So how did the New York Giants sweep *this* team in the World Series?

"It was simple," manager Al Lopez would explain. "We went cold, the breaks went against us, and the Giants played good ball and beat us."

If only it were that simple.

The 1954 Indians were a team that heated up early and stayed hot. At one point, they were 69 games *over* .500. When they clinched the pennant on September 18, a parade from the East Side to the West Side, 18 miles long, hailed the victors.

The Tribe was led by the fearsome Big Four—Bob Feller, Mike Garcia, Bob Lemon, and Early Wynn. Lemon and Wynn each won 23 games, Garcia checked in with 19 wins, and Feller had 13. First-year starter Art Houtteman added 15. In the bullpen, Ray Narleski and Don Mossi provided relief. Catcher Jim Hegan was a respected handler.

At the plate, Larry Doby hit 32 homers and knocked in 126 runs while finishing as the runner-up in MVP voting. Bobby Avila led all AL hitters with a .341 average, and Al Rosen and Vic Wertz supplied more punch.

So how'd they lose?

Game 1 set the tone. Willie Mays's legendary over-the-shoulder grab of Wertz's shot to the deepest regions of the Polo Grounds still breaks the hearts of Clevelanders. It came with two on in the eighth inning and the score tied. At the time, Lemon was sailing, so the runs probably would have assured victory. Instead, the Indians lost in the tenth inning on Dusty Rhodes's pinch-hit, three-run homer.

"For many fans and followers, the entire history of the Indians

Cleveland's Big Four of Bob Lemon, Early Wynn, Bob Feller, and Mike Garcia (left to right) is considered by many the best pitching rotation ever. Collectively they won 915 games, and three made the Hall of Fame. But somehow this fearsome foursome didn't deliver in the 1954 World Series.

The 1954 Indians won 111 games, and fans expected four more in the World Series. The underdog New York Giants made sure that didn't happen as they amazed the baseball world by sweeping the Tribe.

Bobby Avila: El Pionero

Larry Doby wasn't Cleveland's only trailblazer. Bobby Avila, a scrappy second baseman from Mexico, became an Indian in 1949 when few Latinos played in the majors. In 10 years with the Tribe, Avila hit .300 three times and made three All-Star Teams.

Avila's best year was 1954, when he hit an AL-best .341, scored 112 runs, and struck out just 31 times. The spark he added to the Indians lineup led to a third-place finish in MVP voting. Avila was the first of many Latino batting champions, but he was the last Indian player to wear that crown.

Avila's success wasn't limited to the diamond. In retirement, he became mayor of his hometown of Veracruz and was later elected to Mexico's Congress.

Long before The Drive, The Fumble, and The Shot broke hearts in Cleveland, fans suffered through The Catch. Willie Mays's historic grab of Vic Wertz's (*inset*) long drive to no-man's land in the Polo Grounds crushed Cleveland's spirit.

was forever altered by Mays's catch and Rhodes's home run," wrote researcher Morris Eckhouse.

More frustration followed in Game 2. The Indians out-hit the Giants but lost 3–1 as New York ace Johnny Antonelli outgunned Wynn. Down 2–0 in the Series, the Indians saw the fever subside in Cleveland when play shifted to Municipal Stadium. Unlike the 1948 Series when fans packed every seat, a crowd of 71,555 came for Game 3. It was never a game. The Giants led big after six frames and won 6–2.

By Game 4, a white flag flapped in the Lake Erie breeze running through Municipal Stadium. The Giants grabbed a 7–0 lead and held on as the Indians managed four late-inning runs. The Giants had brushed aside the mighty Tribe, leaving a bitter taste lingering in the mouths of Indians fans.

CHAPTER FOUR

The Rocky Road 1955–1968

CURSES! THE YANKEES. The White Sox. Second-place finishes. Herb Score. Rocky Colavito. Trader Frank Lane. Bobby Bragan. Sudden Sam. Curses and cursed, all of them. The 14 years after the 1954 World Series served teaspoons of hard luck, dashes of disappointment, and small portions of excitement. It was too hard to swallow on occasion. Sometimes, Tribe fans felt jinxed; other times, they felt pure betrayal. What they didn't know was that these weren't the worst of times—the ball was just starting to roll uphill.

With his mighty swing and cannon arm, a youthful Rocky Colavito was primed to carry on the Indians' winning tradition when his star landed in Cleveland in 1956. The Rock clubbed 129 homers in his first four full seasons.

Herb Score, ordained as the Tribe's next pitching phenom, recovered from the line drive that struck his face, but he didn't recover his greatness. The injury seemed to epitomize the dawn of four decades of misfortunes that dogged the Indians.

Woulda, Coulda, Shoulda

General Manager Hank Greenberg didn't dismantle the Indians after the gut-wrenching collapse in the 1954 World Series. Despite the graying whiskers of his stars and three second-place finishes in four years, the 1955 Cleveland roster was essentially a mirror of the pennant winners. After all, how far could a team slide after winning 111 games?

Arriving from the Chicago Cubs to man left field was aging slugger Ralph Kiner. Rookie phenom Herb Score joined the Big Four, whose members were now all older than 30.

Pitching was still Cleveland's strength, but the team's offense didn't match its 1954 output. Al Rosen, Larry Doby, and Bobby Avila saw their numbers dramatically decline, and the Tribe lacked enough punch to keep pace. The Indians chased the Yankees all summer and won 93 games, enough to finish three games out.

Bob Feller ended his stellar career after starting the 1956 season 0–4, sending Greenberg to his toolbox for the big work that had to be done. The GM shipped Doby to the

General Manager Frank Lane reshaped the 1959 Indians, and the squad sprinted out of the gate with a 10–1 record. The Tribe spent 64 days in first place before a July swoon put them behind the White Sox for good.

White Sox for shortstop Chico Carrasquel. A rookie outfielder named Rocky Colavito got enough playing time to hit 21 homers.

Score continued his rise, joining Early Wynn and Bob Lemon as 20-game winners. However, when it came to hitting, the Indians were the Boys of Slumber. They batted just .244 and finished second to the Yankees again. That made five second-place finishes in six seasons.

Al Lopez had had enough and resigned. Fans had seen enough, too. Attendance, like the team batting average, was next to last in the AL. Rosen, unhappy with his salary, retired.

After the Indians finished sixth in 1957, Frank Lane replaced Greenberg as general manager and started acquiring speed, hitting, and defense. Lane traded Wynn after the 1957 season, and dealt Avila, Vic Wertz, and relievers Don Mossi and Ray Narleski after Cleveland finished fourth in 1958. In 1959, the Indians, featuring newcomers Minnie Minoso, Vic Power, and Billy Martin to go with Colavito, were back in the hunt. Former second baseman Joe Gordon was managing the club.

Colavito's 42 home runs tied him with Washington's Harmon Killebrew for the league lead, and Tito Francona hit .363 (but he fell short of the minimum number of at-bats to qualify for the batting title). Pitching became the team's Achilles' heel. With Score injured, the Indians had Cal McLish (19 wins), Gary Bell (16 wins), and little else.

The race with Chicago's Go-Go White Sox lasted most of the summer. Ironically, Lopez was Chicago's manager and Greenberg was GM—and their checks were signed by owner Bill Veeck. The race essentially ended in late August when Chicago swept a four-game set in Cleveland, which sent the Tribe reeling. The Indians would finish in second and wouldn't get close again for a long while.

Bob Lemon was 35, but he won 20 games for the 1956 Indians. It would be his last great hurrah on the lakefront; by 1959, the future Hall of Famer was retired.

You Won't See This Today

Ralph Kiner came to Cleveland in 1955 in need of a head exam. After Cleveland traded for the seven-time National League home run champion, a contract dispute ensued.

Kiner didn't want a fatter salary. He wanted *less*.

"Maybe I should go to a psychiatrist," he joked.

Kiner made $65,000 in 1954 during his worst season: 22 homers and 73 RBI. The nine-year veteran insisted on a 40 percent pay cut when the Chicago Cubs traded him to Cleveland. That pay cut was 15 percent more than what was allowable. The Indians needed league permission to meet Kiner's demand.

Hobbled by injuries, Kiner hit just 18 home runs and a career-low .243 for the Indians. Salary was never again an issue. Kiner retired at 32.

HIGH SCHOOL PROSPECT ROGER MARIS, SIGNED BY THE INDIANS IN 1953 FOR $5,000, HIT 23 HOME RUNS FOR CLEVELAND IN 167 GAMES. HE WOULD EARN HIS PLACE IN HISTORY WITH THE YANKEES, FOR WHOM HE HIT A RECORD 61 DINGERS IN 1961.

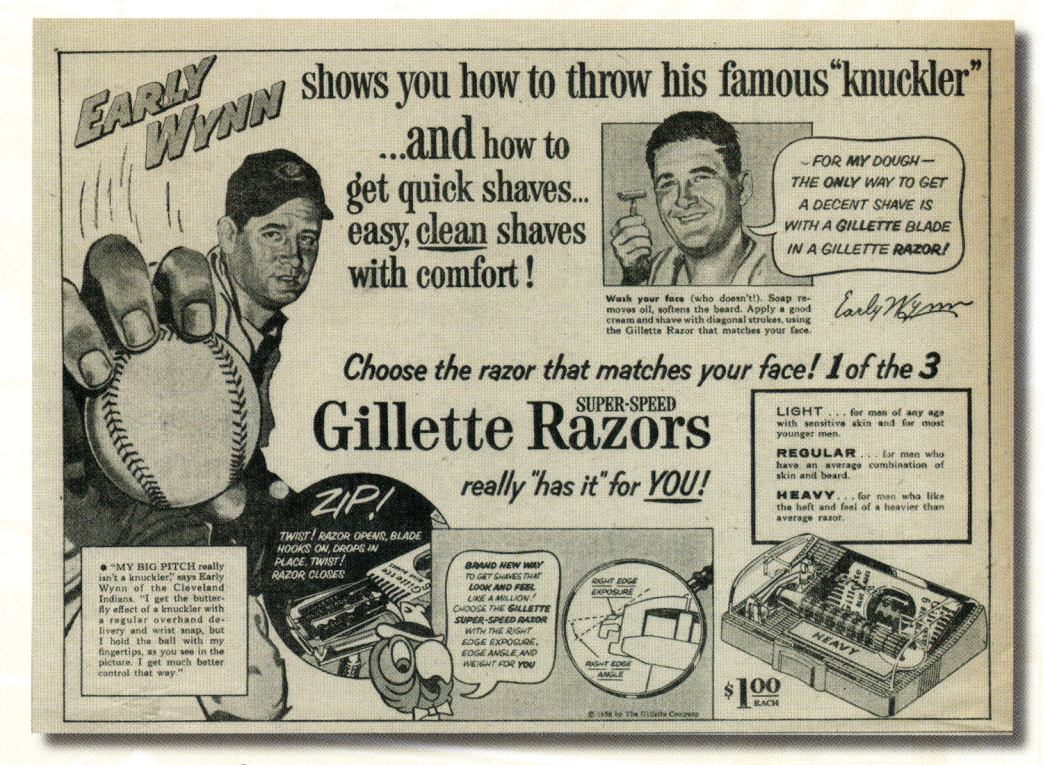

SCORECARDS IN 1955 INCLUDED HERB SCORE'S NAME, BUT THE ROOKIE'S 16 WINS WEREN'T ENOUGH AS THE INDIANS FINISHED SECOND, THREE GAMES BEHIND THE HATED YANKEES.

WITH HELP FROM PITCHING COACH MEL HARDER, EARLY WYNN PERFECTED HIS KNUCKLEBALL AFTER ARRIVING IN CLEVELAND IN A 1948 TRADE WITH WASHINGTON. THE KNUCKLER WAS SO GOOD IT EARNED MENTION IN THIS GILLETTE ADVERTISEMENT.

Colavito Fans Out for Lane's Scalp

Reaction Violent as Trade Stirs Man-in-Street

A majority of Indian fans are on the warpath today. Object: Frank Lane's scalp.

The general manager's bombshell trade of Rocky Colavito for Harvey Kuenn has triggered the biggest man-in-the-street reaction here since Bill Veeck threatened to exile Lou Boudreau from the wigwam in 1947.

And sentiment among those who whirl the turnstiles is overwhelmingly—often violently—against Colavito going to Detroit.

The hundreds of phone calls that yesterday lit up The Press switchboard like a short-circuited pinball machine ran 9-to-1 in opposition to Lane and the deal.

In contrast, there weren't nearly as many protests last September when Lane tried to fire Joe Gordon as manager.

Callers most aroused about Colavito obviously were Rocky's rabid and numerous rooters. In a later sampling of opinion by Press staff members, the ratio of fans knocking the swap dropped to 2-to-1.

From some of the severest critics, however, came threats of ticket cancellations and Stadium boycotts and demands that Lane trade himself out of town.

Here are some samples:

HOWARD BRAXTON, 7602 Hollon: "I was planning on going to tomorrow's opener but won't go now."

R. S. KAPON, 1710 Prospect: "I'm canceling four box seats."

MRS. ALBERT NEUMANN, 3280 W. 84: "I hope Detroit beats the pants off the Indians."

STO COTONE, 1311 W. 69: "What's better than seeing a home run, win or lose?"

CHARLES HERMAN, 3241 E. 135: "Somebody doesn't know much about baseball, meaning Lane. If he was so concerned himself, he wouldn't be jumping from one team to another every few years. This is as bad as trying to get rid of Gordon."

LEONARD BAZELAK, 872 Lecona: "Trade Lane."

ENE KENNEY, 1531 Hillcrest: "Lane's relying too much on Bond taking up the home run slack."

OE KLEIN, 1761 Bellingham: "Kuenn may be good but I still like the long ball. Three singles won't win a game."

NGELO MARSHALL, 5973 Marnell: "I know 10 fans

Turn to Page 39, Column 3

CLEVELAND PRESS ARTIST LOU DARVAS NAILED THE REACTION TO FRANK LANE'S TRADE OF ROCKY COLAVITO.

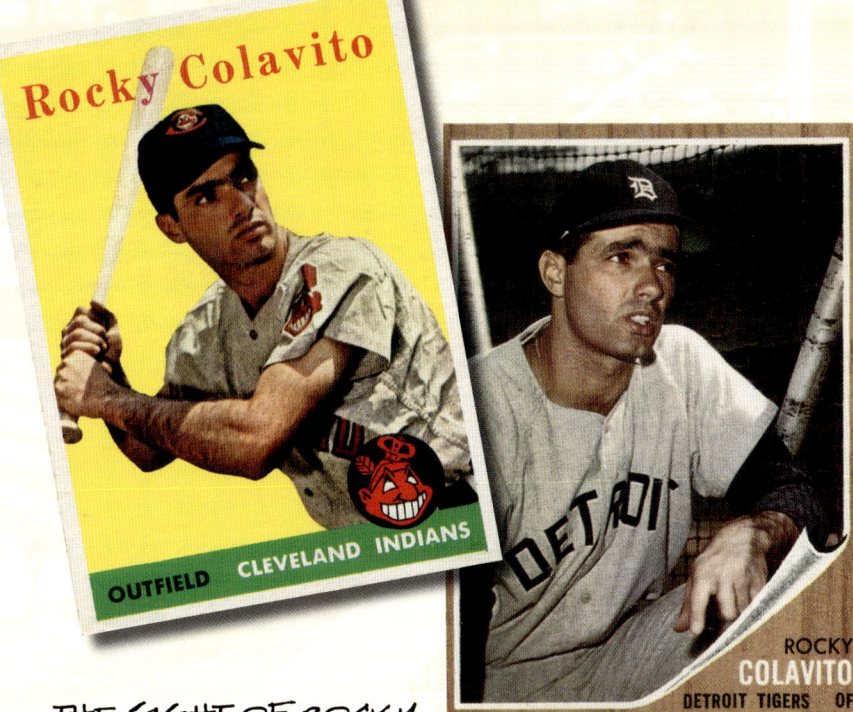

THE SIGHT OF ROCKY COLAVITO IN A TIGERS UNIFORM NAUSEATED INDIANS FANS, BUT THE TRIBE PAID DEARLY TO RETURN THE ROCK TO CLEVELAND IN 1965. THE TEAM GAVE UP THREE PLAYERS, INCLUDING PITCHER TOMMY JOHN.

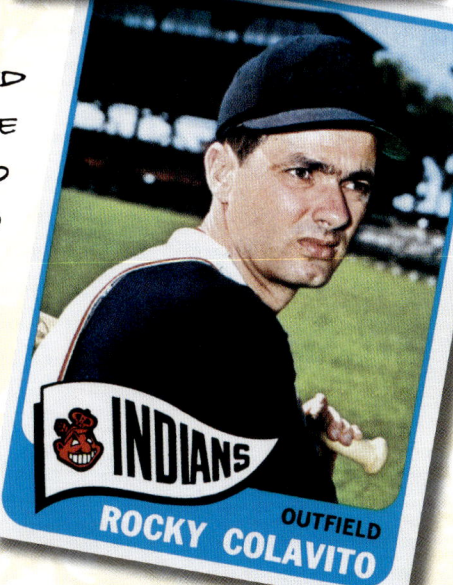

VIC WERTZ OVERCAME POLIO FOLLOWING THE 1954 WORLD SERIES. IN 1956, HE SLAMMED A CAREER-BEST 32 HOME RUNS AND DROVE IN 106 RUNS. HIS COMEBACK EARNED HIM THE CLUB'S MAN OF THE YEAR AWARD.

Score Goes Down

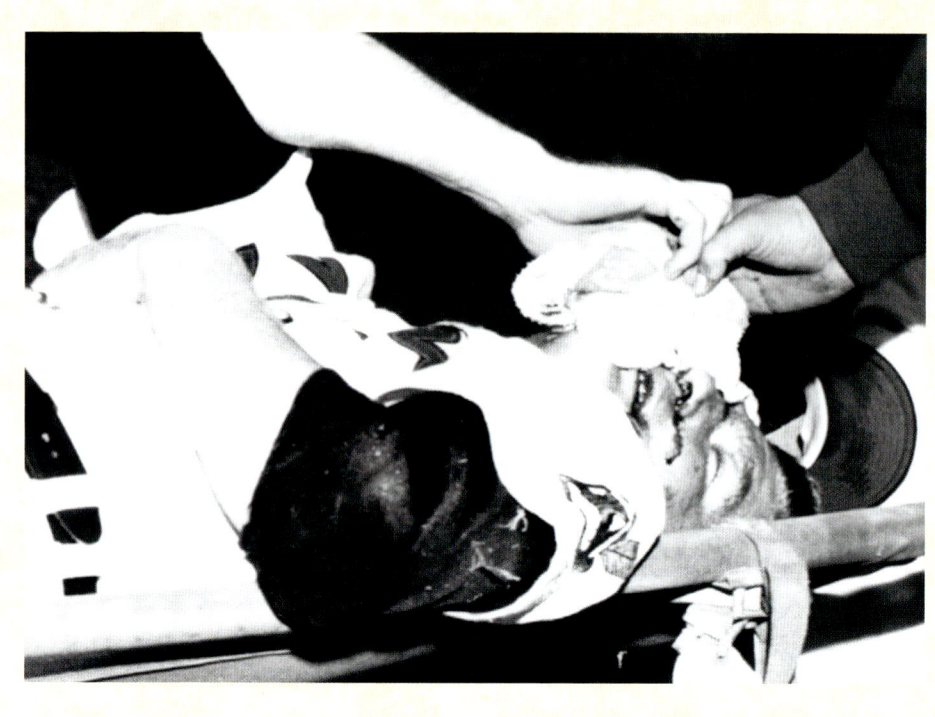

Herb Score was the first rookie in baseball history to strike out more than 200 batters in a season. His 245 Ks in 1955 stood as a major-league rookie record until Dwight Gooden bested that mark in 1984. Indians fans to this day still wonder what could have been.

When Indians scout Cy Slapnicka signed teenager Bob Feller, he called the Iowa farm boy the greatest pitcher he had ever seen. Almost 20 years later, Slapnicka had the same high praise for Herb Score.

Even Tris Speaker oozed in agreement: "If nothing happens to Score, the kid's got to be the greatest."

Score went 16–10 and struck out a rookie-record 245 batters in 1955. He had a 20–9 record and 263 Ks in his second season. Baseball took notice of the 23-year-old two-time All-Star. Before the 1957 season, the Boston Red Sox offered the Indians $1 million for Score's contract. The new Indians owners had just paid $3.9 million for *the entire team.*

"He's not for sale at any price," said GM Hank Greenberg.

Score's career changed on May 7, 1957, when the New York Yankees visited Municipal Stadium. In the first inning, New York third baseman Gil McDougald lined one of Score's fastballs right back up the middle. The rocket shattered Score's right eye socket, putting Cleveland's wunderkind out for the year. Legend claims the injury ruined Score's career. In truth, an arm injury the following spring did more damage. He won only 11 games over the next two seasons.

The Indians traded Score to the White Sox just before the 1960 opener. Score made 27 starts for Chicago before retiring in 1963. He returned to Cleveland in 1964 to broadcast Indians games and stayed with the team for more than 30 years.

The Strongest Bond

Rookie Walter Bond faced the uphill battle of replacing a fan favorite. Tragically, it would not be his greatest challenge.

Bond took over in right field in 1960 after Rocky Colavito was dealt to Detroit. Hate letters and a .221 average in 40 games dogged the 22-year-old. Bond didn't blame salty Indians fans, but, he said, "I didn't trade [Colavito]."

A leukemia diagnosis in 1962 sidetracked Bond, but he continued to chase major-league glory while fighting the disease over the next five years. Bond hit 20 home runs for Houston in 1964 and was hitting .313 through 10 games with Minnesota before leaving the team due to his illness. He died on September 14, 1967, at age 29.

Planet Piersall

He fought with fans, teammates, managers, umpires, and reporters, but Jimmy Piersall also tormented himself. In 1959, the zany outfielder with bipolar disorder came to Cleveland, where he put up some of his best stats and had some of his greatest meltdowns.

"You couldn't dislike Jimmy," Rocky Colavito said. "He was fun."

In a game against Boston, Piersall ran around the outfield flapping his arms, trying to distract the great Ted Williams. Piersall was thrown out of the game after refusing an umpire's order to stop. Piersall charged the ump, but his teammates kept him from reaching his target. On another occasion, he sat atop Municipal Stadium's outfield fence shooting the breeze with fans. Another time Piersall spread his arms out like an airplane as he ran to first base.

Piersall talked incessantly, to whomever was around, even to the monuments at Yankee Stadium. He'd sing a tune to himself as he dug into the batter's box. Acting crazy became his shtick.

Piersall broke into the majors in 1952 with the Boston Red Sox. He came up as a top-flight outfielder with superior defensive skills who was also a consistent hitter. In fact, Williams would say he was one of the best outfielders in the game. But Piersall, whose mother had a mental illness, suffered a nervous breakdown that season. He turned his inner turmoil into a top-selling book, *Fear Strikes Out*, which was later made into a movie in 1957 that starred Anthony Perkins as Piersall and Karl Malden as his father, John.

"Probably the best thing that happened to me was going nuts," Piersall later wrote. "Whoever heard of Jimmy Piersall until that happened?"

Indians GM Frank Lane traded for Piersall in 1959. Straight-arrow manager Joe Gordon clashed often with the unpredictable outfielder. Gordon was out by the next season, but Piersall stayed.

After a lackluster first year in Cleveland, Piersall rebounded to hit .282 with 18 homers in 1960. The following season, he hit .322. When Lane was shown the door, the Piersall sideshow ended its run in Cleveland when the Indians traded him to Washington.

Jimmy Piersall cashed in on his mental illness, entertaining fans with his wild antics and giving hecklers plenty of ammunition. He's seen here holding golf balls, a tape measure, a hairbrush, and other items that Detroit fans threw at him during a game at Tiger Stadium.

Indian Giver

There is perhaps no greater villain in Indians history than Frank Lane. His three-year tenure as general manager, however, was not all bad.

Seriously.

When "Trader" Lane arrived after the 1957 season, he inherited a sixth-place team that couldn't draw flies. He brought a winning résumé from stints as GM of the White Sox and Cardinals and an ego to boot. In fact, while with St. Louis, Lane contemplated trading Stan Musial. The GM went about reshaping the Indians with a flurry of trades. In two seasons, he picked up Minnie Minoso, Billy Martin, Vic Power, Woodie Held, and Jimmy Piersall.

He brought in Joe Gordon, a hero from the Indians' 1948 World Series team, to replace manager Bobby Bragan in the middle of the 1958 season. The story goes that Bragan was so angry that he cast a curse on the Indians, a notion he denies.

However, by 1959, the Indians were in a pennant race. Attendance shot up to nearly 1.5 million. Clevelanders were once again in love with their Indians.

In his time with the Indians, "Frantic Frank" made 50 transactions involving 112 players. History doesn't reflect well on many of his moves. For instance, he traded Norm Cash for Steve Demeter. Cash would spend 17 years in the majors and smash 377 homers. Demeter batted five times for the Tribe. Lane also traded a young prospect named Roger Maris. No one was safe with Lane in charge. He even swapped managers with Detroit, a baseball first, sending Gordon to Michigan for Jimmy Dykes.

But the most obscene move came just before Opening Day 1960. Lane traded Rocky Colavito, the most beloved Indian since Lou Boudreau, to Detroit for AL batting champion Harvey Kuenn, who would spend only one season in Cleveland. Predictably, the Indians tumbled to fourth place. Attendance followed suit.

Fans never forgave Lane. His tenure ended in January 1961. Years later, Lane insisted the Colavito-Kuenn trade was a good one.

"I'd still trade that [expletive] fruit peddler for Kuenn," he said.

Unfortunately, the Cleveland faithful ended up with all the sour grapes.

Joe Gordon (*right*), a hero of the 1948 Indians, feuded often with general manager Frank Lane while managing the 1959 team. The following summer, Lane pulled the unthinkable: He traded Gordon to Detroit for manager Jimmy Dykes.

Rock Rolled Out of Town

He had it all: power, a rocket throwing arm, a catchy name, leading-man looks, and charm. Rocky Colavito *was* Cleveland.

The Rock averaged nearly 30 home runs and more than 90 RBI in his four seasons as Cleveland's right fielder. He was a home-grown product of the Indians farm system who came up to stay in 1956. Colavito was 6'3" and full of muscle. Men admired him, kids emulated him, and women adored him.

On June 10, 1959, Colavito pumped out home runs in four consecutive at-bats, tying a major-league record and bringing Orioles fans to their feet in Baltimore's Memorial Stadium. Life was good in Cleveland: Colavito shared the AL home run title with Washington's Harmon Killebrew (42), and the Indians were a contender. *Time* magazine even put the Rock on the cover.

The gut punch came two days before the 1960 season started when Frank Lane traded Colavito to Detroit for Harvey Kuenn. Colavito took right field for the Tigers on Opening Day in Cleveland. The sight was unbearable and unforgivable.

In an attempt to win back fans, the Tribe traded to get a fading Colavito back five years later. The cost was eventual 288-game winner Tommy John and outfielder (and Miracle Mets hero) Tommie Agee. Still, Colavito retains a spot in the hearts of Cleveland fans; in 1975, they voted the Rock their most memorable Indian.

Young fans imitated his batting stance, older fans embraced his sprints to right field after every inning, and women swooned over his Hollywood good looks. Without a doubt, Rocky Colavito was Cleveland's favorite son.

What's in a Name?

With a name like Power, grace doesn't spring to mind, but that's exactly what Vic Power brought to the Indians. Power used his soft hands and wide range to win four of his seven consecutive Gold Glove Awards while handling first base for the Indians from 1958 to 1961. Although Power had little pop (126 career home runs), he did have a career batting average of .284.

Further contradicting his name is the fact that he tied a major-league record by stealing home twice in a 1958 game against Detroit. He stole home earlier that season while with Kansas City. They were his only swipes of the year.

Red Ink and Empty Seats

The Indians' glory days were in the rearview mirror by 1963. Fans avoided Municipal Stadium in droves, and the team's attendance, once the envy of clubs everywhere, was now among the lowest in baseball. The team's record corresponded almost perfectly, as the Indians hovered in the southern half of the American League standings.

Beginning in the late 1950s, team ownership by large groups of Cleveland investors was constantly in flux and always short on cash. Three syndicates in all ran the team after owner Bill Veeck sold out in 1949. Scouts assigned to unearth talented commodities were cut to save money. Minor-league affiliates shrunk in numbers. The team's bottom line was bright red, and its stadium lease with the city didn't help. Threats of relocating the Indians to Oakland, Seattle, Minneapolis, Houston, or Dallas were more than rumors.

The future looked grim—for the franchise and for the city.

Gabe Paul headed the consortium that took over the Indians in 1963. At least he respected the city's baseball history.

"I absolutely always thought Cleveland was a good baseball town, that all the fans ever needed was a winning team," he said.

After the damage GM Frank Lane inflicted, hosting the 1963 All-Star Game was supposed to spark life into the ailing franchise. Instead, it provided a national stage for a team in disarray and its apathetic fan base.

The 1963 All-Star Game was supposed to generate interest in Cleveland baseball, but despite the ads and hoopla, fans filled barely half of the cavernous Municipal Stadium.

The Midsummer Classic was overexposed: Eight All-Star Games had been played in the preceding four summers. Municipal Stadium seemed a logical choice for returning the game to its past spotlight splendor; after all, 69,751 fans had watched the 1954 game when it was played in Cleveland. Times had changed, though. Cleveland fans, it seems, sent a message as only 44,160 showed for the game, leaving more than 30,000 seats empty.

Exclusive Club Gets Early Addition

With the Indians wallowing in the standings and at the gate by mid-June 1963, an over-the-hill Early Wynn returned to Cleveland, one win shy of 300 career victories. Wynn, 43, looked as if he were attending an old-timers game when he was welcomed by his new teammates.

Early Wynn was as tenacious a pitcher as they came, a fierce competitor who staked his claim to the inside of home plate. They say even his mother, if she dared crowd the plate, wouldn't escape his wrath.

"I've got a right to knock down anybody holding a bat," Wynn told author Roger Kahn.

Wynn won 300 games in a 23-year career that spanned parts of four decades. He had two tours with the Indians, winning 20 or more games four times over 10 seasons. Acquiring him in 1948 from the Washington Senators was one of the best trades in Indians history. Trading him in 1957 to the Chicago White Sox was one of the worst. Wynn won the 1959 Cy Young Award while leading the White Sox to the pennant. He beat the second-place Indians six times.

Chicago released Wynn and his 299 career victories in 1962. The 43-year-old signed as a free agent with Cleveland for the next season. The Indians were happy to take him—team management saw Wynn's pursuit of 300 wins as a draw for a team with plenty of places to sit.

Wynn made five starts before winning No. 300 on July 13 in Kansas City. He pitched five innings and let the bullpen save his milestone win. Wynn then became a relief pitcher and retired at season's end. His next stop was the Hall of Fame, which he entered in 1972.

Tomahawk Pop

Woodie Held—gone. Pedro Ramos—outtahere. Tito Francona—blast off. Larry Brown—bye-bye, baseball. Four hitters, four homers, all hit off one unfortunate relief pitcher, Paul Foytack of the Los Angeles Angels. Most fans only read about the deluge because just 7,288 came to Municipal Stadium on July 31, 1963, to see a major-league pitcher give up four consecutive home runs for the first time in history. Ramos, the Indians' starting pitcher, homered twice and struck out 15 in Cleveland's 9–5 win.

The Cleveland Press Collection, Cleveland State University Library/Lou Darvas

Sports Illustrated — JUNE 3, 1963 — 25 CENTS

BOB HOPE OF THE CLEVELAND INDIANS

BOB HOPE GREW UP IN CLEVELAND AND BECAME A MINORITY OWNER OF THE TRIBE WHEN BILL VEECK BOUGHT THE INDIANS. HOPE OFTEN APPEARED WEARING AN INDIANS UNIFORM AND MAINTAINED A SMALL STAKE IN THE CLUB FOR YEARS.

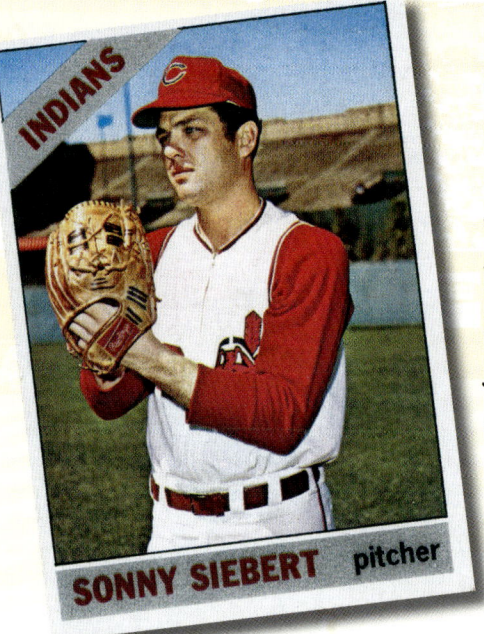

SONNY SIEBERT — pitcher

ONLY 10,469 FANS SAW SONNY SIEBERT'S JUNE 10, 1966, NO-HITTER AGAINST THE WASHINGTON SENATORS AT MUNICIPAL STADIUM. SIEBERT WALKED JUST ONE WHILE STRIKING OUT SEVEN. HE HAD A PAIR OF 16-WIN SEASONS FOR THE TRIBE.

THE CRANE POTATO CHIP COMPANY CREATED ITS OWN VERSION OF CHIEF WAHOO FOR THIS PIN-BACK GIVEAWAY FROM THE 1960S.

CLEVELAND INDIANS

1964 ROOKIE STARS INDIANS — TOMMY JOHN PITCHER — BOB CHANCE OUTFIELD

TOMMY JOHN WON TWO GAMES FOR THE INDIANS AFTER ARRIVING IN 1963—HE WON 286 GAMES ELSEWHERE. BOB CHANCE HIT 14 HOME RUNS IN 1964 BEFORE FADING INTO OBSCURITY.

SAM CALLS IT:

'Best Four Innings of My Life'

By BOB SUDYK

How long will it be until Sam McDowell breaks Bob Feller's and Sandy Koufax's major league record of 18 strikeouts in a single game?

"When a pitcher has it all going for him there isn't anything he can't do," said the 23-year-old southpaw, who left 11,466 fans gasping yesterday in Detroit while he fanned 13 batters in the first five innings.

McDOWELL WAS ONLY six strikeouts and four innings away from a new nine-inning mark when his left shoulder began to scream in protest. He breezed one more batter in the sixth, gave up a couple of hits and informed manager George Strickland at the end of the inning about his shoulder miseries.

"I might have been able to get through the rest of the game. I told George my arm was tiring so he'd know, and he said, 'Okay, that's it'," said McDowell, who wanted to try at least one more inning.

Sonny Siebert, whose sore arm may keep him out of tomorrow night's opener against Minnesota, said flatly, "Sam would have broken the strikeout record easy, if his shoulder hadn't acted up. He'll do it eventually."

McDOWELL LOOKED DOWN at his left arm, which on sight looks pretty much like anybody else's, and said, "Those were the best four innings of my life . . . If just one game, my arm wouldn't start aching enough to stop me from throwing hard, maybe I'd win one." He was replaced by John O'Donoghue and Luis Tiant, who finally won it in the 10th inning, 6-5.

The Sudden One fanned nine of the first 10 batters he faced. He tied a major league record by breezing the first five. Mickey Stanley, the sixth Detroit batter, slapped a double to interrupt the whiff string.

Strickland will stay with the Kiddie Korps of first baseman Bill Davis, second baseman Vern Fuller and Jose Vidal in place of Rocky Colavito. "I see no reason to change," said Strick, "we're doing better than we did before."

VIC DAVALILLO's two-run homer off Denny McLain headlined the Indians' five runs in the fourth and fifth innings. Detroit tied it on pinch-hitting Norm Cash's three-run homer in the eighth. Then came Max Alvis' two-out single in the 10th, scoring Davalillo, who had doubled.

The Cleveland Press Collection, Cleveland State University Library

SAM MCDOWELL SEEMED DESTINED TO BREAK BASEBALL'S SINGLE-GAME STRIKEOUT RECORD OF 18 AFTER FANNING 14 THROUGH SIX INNINGS IN A GAME AGAINST THE TIGERS IN 1966. MANAGER GEORGE STRICKLAND, HOWEVER, REMOVED MCDOWELL TO PROTECT THE PITCHER'S AILING SHOULDER.

THE TERMINAL TOWER AND MUNICIPAL STADIUM, SEEN HERE ON THIS 1960S STICKER, SERVED AS CLEVELAND LANDMARKS AND DESTINATION LOCATIONS TO RESIDENTS AND VISITORS BEGINNING IN THE EARLY 1930S.

THIRD BASEMAN MAX ALVIS, WHO HIT 22 HOMERS AS A ROOKIE IN 1963, OVERCAME SPINAL MENINGITIS THE FOLLOWING SUMMER TO MAKE THE 1965 AL ALL-STAR TEAM.

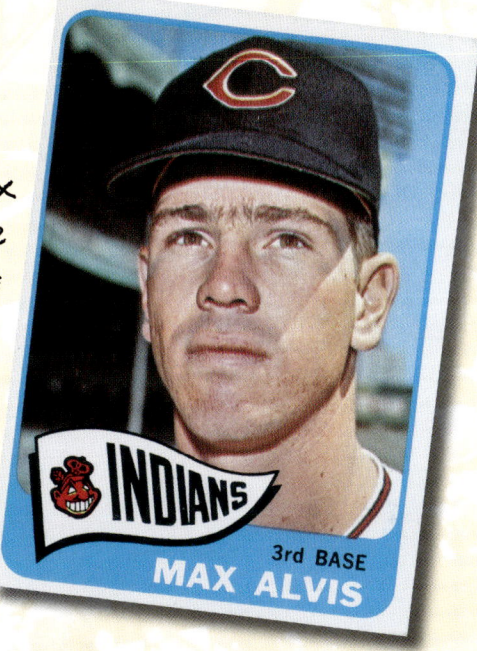

The Cuban Whirlwind

Across baseball, 1968 was the year of the pitcher. In Cleveland, the season belonged to Luis Tiant. "El Tiante" went 21–9 for the Tribe, striking out 264 batters while fashioning an Addie Joss–like 1.60 ERA, best in the AL.

Tiant's whirling, back-to-home-plate, head-to-the-stars delivery often confounded hitters. Such was the case when he threw 10 shutout innings and logged a club-record 19 strikeouts against the Minnesota Twins on July 3. He started the All-Star Game for the AL six days later.

"It was fun playing behind him," said Indians third baseman Max Alvis. "He had bulldog competitiveness."

The only son of Negro Leagues star Luis Tiant, Sr., "Looie" was a product of the Indians farm system, a find in Cuba by former Indian-turned-scout Bobby Avila. El Tiante debuted in 1964, shutting out the mighty Yankees on four hits while fanning 11. Tiant was decent for four years before blossoming in 1968. However, the following season was a reversal of fortune as Tiant went 9–20 and the Indians traded him to the Twins in a six-player deal that brought Graig Nettles to Cleveland. The Twins released Tiant after one season, seemingly ending his career.

Looie was resurrected after a tryout with the Red Sox the next year. In Boston, he won 20 games three times on his way to a 19-year career during which he collected 229 victories.

Luis Tiant had a simple explanation for pitching: "If you have luck, you win." On July 3, 1968, Lady Luck smiled on El Tiante, as he struck out 19 batters in a 10-inning game against Minnesota.

Streaking to Mediocrity

The Indians sprinted from the gate in 1966, winning their first 10 games to set an AL record. That was the good news. After 87 wins the previous year, the most since 1959, some Indians fans were entertaining pennant dreams.

The bad news was that the Baltimore Orioles won nine of their first 10. So, when Chicago snapped the Indians' streak in front of 13,023 at Municipal Stadium, the Tribe found themselves merely tied for the AL lead.

Cleveland's record went to 14–1, and the team clung to first place through May before cooling. The Orioles never chilled. By season's end, the Indians stumbled to 81–81 to finish fifth, 17 games behind the O's.

Major League Standings

AMERICAN LEAGUE

	W	L	Pct.	GB
INDIANS	10	0	1.000	—
Baltimore	9	1	.900	1
Chicago	9	3	.750	2
Detroit	10	4	.717	2
California	6	6	.500	5
Minnesota	4	6	.400	6
Boston	3	9	.250	8
Washington	3	9	.250	8
Kansas City	2	9	.182	8½
New York	2	11	.154	9½

NATIONAL LEAGUE

	W	L	Pct.	GB
Pittsburgh	10	4	.717	—
San Francisco	10	6	.625	1
Los Angeles	10	6	.625	1
Atlanta	9	7	.563	2
Philadelphia	6	5	.545	2½
Houston	8	8	.500	3
St. Louis	6	8	.429	4
New York	4	6	.400	4
Cincinnati	3	9	.250	6
Chicago	3	10	.231	6½

Sudden Rise, Sudden Fall

Tribe fans never saw the demons lurking inside "Sudden" Sam McDowell. All they saw was the blur of his fastball that conjured thoughts of a left-handed reincarnation of Bob Feller.

McDowell was a hulking 6'5", with an imposing array of fastballs and curves that struck fear into flailing hitters. His wildness at 100 mph only made him scarier. He'd toy with batters, throwing off-speed pitches when he grew bored with his torrid fastball.

"Nobody in the majors could throw faster than Sudden Sam," wrote Cleveland sportswriter Hal Lebovitz.

McDowell was a high school star when the Indians signed him in 1960. He made his major-league debut the following season when he was 18, pitching six-plus innings of shutout baseball while striking out five.

After his first look at the rookie, Twins outfielder Jim Lemon said, "His fastball sure gets up there all of a sudden." McDowell now had a memorable nickname to go with his memorable stuff.

McDowell's wildness kept him from being a regular in the Indians rotation until 1964. He announced his presence with authority the following season, posting a 17-win, 325-strikeout performance. Sudden Sam would top the league in strikeouts five times while making six All-Star teams. McDowell's best year came in 1970 when he won 20 games and struck out 304 for an Indians team that won just 76 games.

But behind the blazing fastball and gaudy stats was an ugly secret that reporters of McDowell's day helped hide: Sudden Sam was a raging alcoholic. McDowell was as relentless in bars as he was on the mound—and often meaner. Barroom brawls were common.

The Indians, seeing a swift decline in McDowell, traded their top pitcher in 1971 to San Francisco for Gaylord Perry. Sudden Sam was suddenly out of baseball by 1975.

"Baseball was easy for me," McDowell said in retirement. "But life was hard."

McDowell tossed four one-hitters while with the Tribe, but he won 20 games just once. His ERA was below 3.00 in six of his eight seasons as a starter.

"Sudden" Sam McDowell was the Randy Johnson of his day. The tall left-hander intimidated AL hitters with his wildness, but he also led the circuit in strikeouts five times from 1965 to 1970.

77

CHAPTER FIVE

The Lost Tribe
1969–1993

A nation looked on as another color barrier was broken in Cleveland with the naming of Frank Robinson as manager in 1975. AL trailblazer and former Indian Larry Doby became the second African American major-league manager when he took over the Chicago White Sox in 1978.

CLEVELAND WAS BLESSED just to have baseball, even lousy baseball. After years of wallowing in losses on the field and in the balance sheets, threats of relocating the franchise were heard nearly every year. Any hope of better days was thrashed as promising ballplayers came and went, for various, almost sickening reasons. The depleted farm system was devoid of promise, thanks to penny-pinching owners. Municipal Stadium, once filled with civic promise, had grown old, cold, and empty. This team needed help. Its fans needed help. No one knew they would have to wait so long to get it.

Bottles, firecrackers, batteries, and chairs, like the one that struck and bloodied the head of Indians reliever Tom Hilgendorf, were tossed onto the field by drunken Tribe fans during the infamous cheap beer promotion at Municipal Stadium in 1974. The riot was another hit to Cleveland's national reputation.

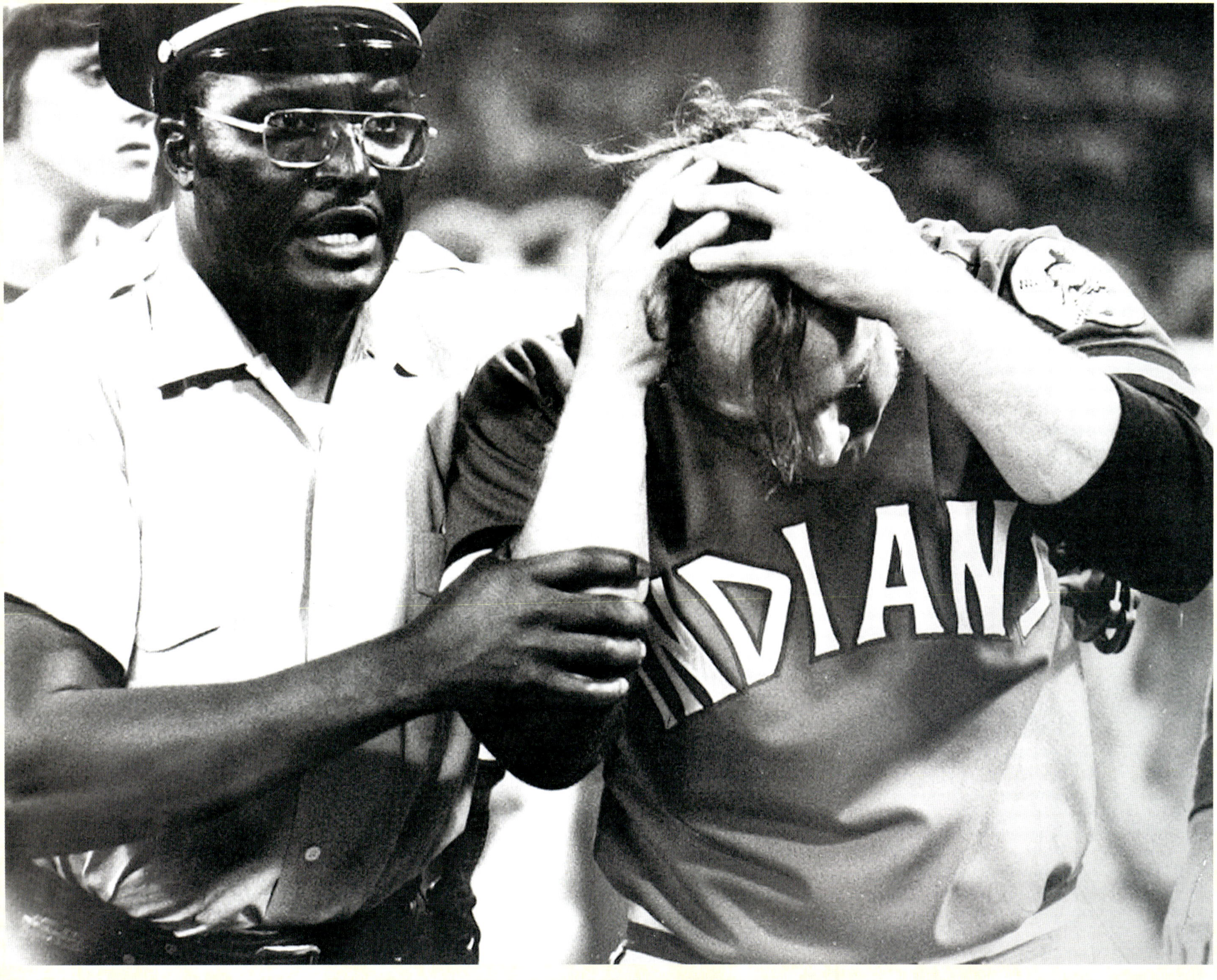
IDIAN

Drawing in Fans

When he stood, he was barely 5'5". Sitting at his drawing board, however, Lou Darvas was a giant, garnering national acclaim as a sports cartoonist.

Darvas catapulted to the top of his profession in the 1940s, when sports legends needed help to spring off the black-and-white page. Cartoonists were newspaper staples, and they enjoyed an age of prominence by capturing images and emotions that eluded photographers.

Darvas, a native Clevelander, began his cartoonist career with the *Cleveland Press* in 1938 when he was 25 years old. His work was so impressive that in 1946 he became a regular contributor to *The Sporting News*, drawing portraits for cover stories and for inside features until the late 1960s. Darvas's style was to draw lifelike portraits that often included humorous smaller cartoons on the side. Sometimes his images were biting, sometimes they were full of rah-rah cheerleading for the home team, but they always evoked emotions from readers, until he put down his pencil in 1973.

To illustrate the Cleveland fan base's livid reaction to Frank Lane's Rocky Colavito trade in 1960, Darvas cast the indifferent general manager as "Little Red Riding Lane" singing, "Who's afraid of the big bad wolves" while passing through darkened woods that were filled with angry fans.

Darvas won national recognition for his sports drawings in 1964 and 1968 from the National Cartoonist Society. Baseball always figured prominently in Darvas's art, and for him, a single play in baseball captured the game's allure.

"For me," he said, "the double play in baseball had just about everything the artist can hope to express... drama, beauty, and simplicity of line for his drawings."

Lou Darvas was inducted into the Sports Media Association of Cleveland and Ohio Hall of Fame for his work as a cartoonist with the old *Cleveland Press*.

Lights Out

They called catcher Ray Fosse "Mule" because he protected home plate with rugged stubbornness. That grittiness is why history remembers Fosse for a single grainy flash that didn't count in the standings but had far-reaching effects.

Fosse was the first-ever pick by the Indians when the amateur draft debuted in 1965. He was projected to be so good that the Indians chose Mule over another catching prospect—Johnny Bench. Fosse blossomed in the summer of 1970, batting .325 with 16 homers heading into the All-Star break. Cleveland's Mule and Sam McDowell were easy picks for the midsummer classic to be played at Cincinnati's new Riverfront Stadium.

The exhibition game went to extra innings, and in the 12th, it happened. Cincinnati's Pete Rose was on second when Chicago Cub Jim Hickman lined a single to center, sending Rose home with the winning run. The throw sailed over Fosse's head, and Charlie Hustle bulldozed Mule, fracturing his left shoulder. Fosse's batting stroke would never be the same; he hit only two more dingers in 1970, and he never hit more than 12 in any season after that.

"Could I have hit 30 home runs a year if that doesn't happen?" Fosse asked. "Maybe not. I'll never know."

Fosse won two Gold Gloves before the Indians traded him in 1973 to Oakland, where he played for two World Series–winning teams. He returned to Cleveland for the 1976 season, a shadow of his former self.

Indians catcher Ray Fosse and Reds outfielder Pete Rose met for dinner the night before the 1970 All-Star Game in Cincinnati. The two had a different kind of meeting at home plate the following night in a collision that has become an iconic baseball moment.

Golly!

For a time, Harold "Gomer" Hodge was the only 4.000 hitter in baseball history. So maybe his math skills matched his baseball talent, but there's a reason Indians fans remember the affable, slack-jawed Tar Heel, who earned his nickname for his resemblance to TV's Gomer Pyle.

Hodge—a 27-year-old infielder—got his only taste of the big leagues in 1971. He began his memorable April with hits in his first four at-bats.

"Golly, fellas, I'm hitting 4.000," he told head-scratching reporters.

Gomer's "average" wouldn't hold. Hodge got 83 at-bats as a pinch-hitter and utility infielder, and he finished the year hitting .205. His one career home run sailed out of Boston's Fenway Park over the fabled Green Monster.

The Nick of Time

Excuse the oversize shades, the full-length mink coats, and the screaming checkered leisure suits. Nick Mileti, as overstated as his wardrobe, was Cleveland's latest baseball savior. If nothing else, Mileti and his pocket of promises kept the Indians in Cleveland.

The lawyer, a "gutsy Sicilian" from Cleveland's East Side, and eight investors bought the franchise in 1972 for nearly $10 million. The sale came as owner Vernon Stouffer, light in the wallet despite the heaping helpings of frozen dinners bearing his name, was ready to play 30 Indians "home" games in the New Orleans Superdome. Fans feared the proposal was merely a prelude to a permanent move to the Big Easy.

"I had no choice but to buy them," Mileti recalled. "They're a Cleveland team, they needed to stay in Cleveland."

Mileti also owned the National Basketball Association's Cleveland Cavaliers, the American Hockey League's Cleveland Barons, and the Cleveland Arena. His investment group outbid another syndicate led by Cleveland shipping magnate George Steinbrenner and former Indian Al Rosen.

Mileti quashed the split-home schedule idea, boasting that the Indians were now among the best-financed teams in the league. There was little truth to his bravado. In two seasons with Mileti serving as chief operating officer, the club lost $2 million. Investors, of which there were 41 by 1975, kicked in more cash, as Mileti surrendered the day-to-day operation of the club to take on lesser roles.

Shortly after taking over the Indians, Nick Mileti, seen here with Gaylord Perry, bragged that the team was "the best financed club in the major leagues." But baseball writer Russell Schneider and others discovered that the Indians were on the opposite end of the financial spectrum.

Chambliss Gets His Shot

Fate opened doors for Chris Chambliss in 1971, as the blue-chip prospect took over first base for the Indians. He responded to the unexpected opportunity with a Rookie of the Year season.

Fate's first victim was Tony Horton, who succumbed to mental pressures and quit baseball in the middle of a doubleheader on August 28, 1970. Ken "Hawk" Harrelson, who was recovering from a broken ankle, opened the 1971 season as Horton's replacement at first. Harrelson's lingering injury and a .199 average prompted the Indians to call up Chambliss, a first-round draft pick in 1970.

Chambliss took over on May 29 and never looked back. He hit .275 with nine home runs and 48 RBI and earned the Rookie of the Year Award.

The Ones Who Got Away

Graig Nettles, Chris Chambliss, Dick Tidrow, Pedro Guerrero, Buddy Bell, and Dennis Eckersley. Sounds like the makings of a pretty good ballclub, right? Cleveland fans wouldn't know. The Indians traded away all that talent in the 1970s. The New York Yankees benefited the most, receiving half of the infield that helped them win the World Series in 1977 and 1978.

Gabe Paul, who ran the Indians for much of the 1960s as president and GM, knew his blue-chippers. When he left to become president and GM for the Yankees in 1973, he began working over new Indians general manager Phil Seghi to acquire Nettles and Chambliss.

In 1972, the Indians traded Nettles and a backup catcher for outfielder Charlie Spikes, catcher John Ellis, and two journeymen. Nettles made five All-Star Teams and won two Gold Gloves while helping the Yankees win two World Series titles. Spikes hit 45 homers his first two seasons in Cleveland before the bottom fell out of his career.

Undaunted, Seghi went back to the Yankees in 1974, trading Chambliss and Tidrow for pitchers Fritz Peterson, Steve Kline, Tom Buskey, and Fred Beene. Yankees fans will never forget the 1976 ALCS home run Chambliss hit against Kansas City to put the Yankees in the World Series. Indians fans would rather forget the whole deal.

But Seghi wasn't done.

Eckersley, a rookie sensation in 1975, pitched a no-hitter for the Tribe in 1977. Eck's marital problems and the Indians' feeling that his sidearm delivery forecasted a short pitching career prompted the Tribe to trade him to Boston in 1978. Eckersley went on to enjoy a 24-season Hall of Fame career. The Indians received third baseman flop Ted Cox, catcher Bo Diaz, and two mediocre pitchers.

Guerrero would go on to tear up National League pitching after the Indians traded him as a minor-league prospect to the Los Angeles Dodgers in 1974 for reliever Bruce Ellingsen, who pitched all of 16 games in Cleveland. Even the beloved Bell wasn't safe. In a curious trade of third basemen, Seghi dealt Bell to Texas in 1978 for Toby Harrah. Although Harrah was steady, Bell went on to win six Gold Gloves. The Indians went on to win nothing.

GM Gabe Paul (*above*) might have saved the Indians from moving, but when he became president and GM of the Yankees, he looted Cleveland's top talent, including Chris Chambliss and Graig Nettles. Paul's successor, Phil Seghi, kept the door open, trading future Gold Glove third baseman Buddy Bell (*top right*) and future Hall of Fame pitcher Dennis Eckersley (*bottom right*).

Getting a ticket to an Indians game became a challenge in the 1990s, but the pickings were thick in the days when Duke Sims, Richie Scheinblum, and Vern Fuller played in Municipal Stadium.

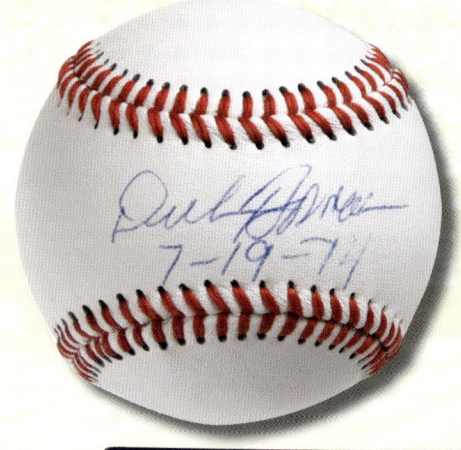

Dick Bosman pitched his July 19, 1974, no-hitter at home against the Oakland A's. Bosman came within one error—his own—of tossing a perfect game.

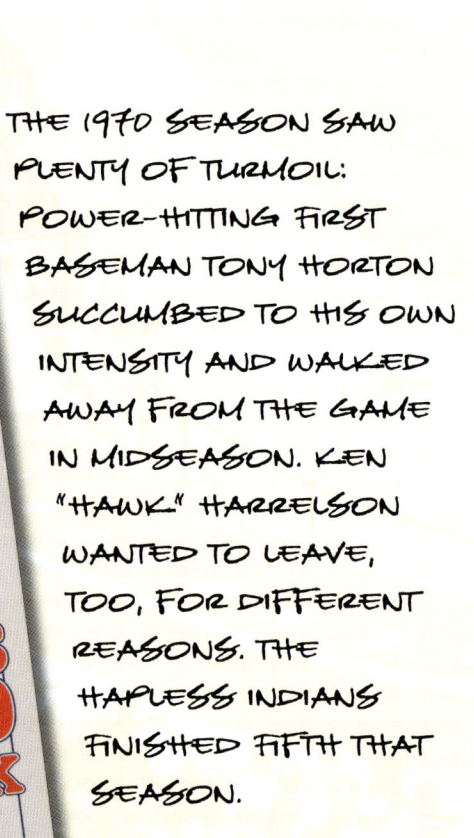

The 1970 season saw plenty of turmoil: power-hitting first baseman Tony Horton succumbed to his own intensity and walked away from the game in midseason. Ken "Hawk" Harrelson wanted to leave, too, for different reasons. The hapless Indians finished fifth that season.

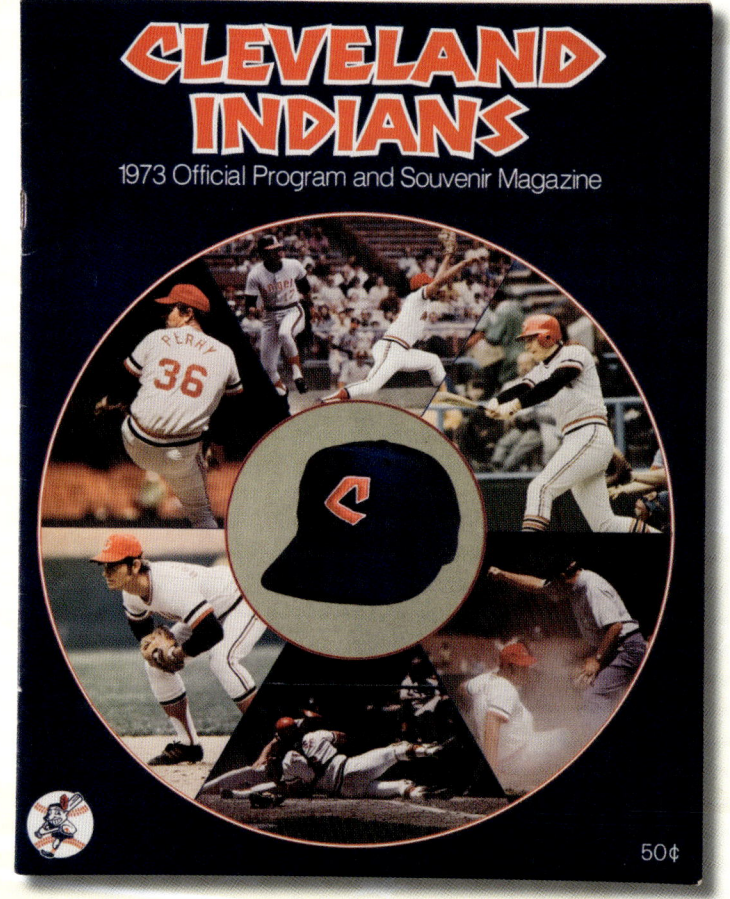

The 1973 team featured the hitting exploits of Oscar Gamble, Charlie Spikes, Walt "No Neck" Williams, and "Silent" George Hendrick, but they went 71-91 due to poor pitching depth.

CLEVELAND INDIANS

A NEW LOGO DIDN'T CHANGE THE INDIANS' STANDING IN THE AMERICAN LEAGUE EASTERN DIVISION. THE CROOKED "C" LETTERING PRECEDED THE GAUDY ALL-RED UNIFORMS THAT SOMEONE SAID MADE BARREL-CHESTED BOOG POWELL LOOK LIKE A FIRE ENGINE ROUNDING THIRD.

JOHN ELLIS WAS THE INDIANS' FIRST DESIGNATED HITTER. A 1973 OPENING DAY CROWD OF 74,420 AT MUNICIPAL STADIUM SAW ELLIS GO A PITCHER-LIKE 0-FOR-4 IN A WIN OVER THE TIGERS.

GAYLORD PERRY, DESPITE HIS REPUTATION AND THE CONSTANT SCRUTINY, WAS NEVER CAUGHT TOSSING A SPITBALL DURING HIS TENURE WITH THE INDIANS.

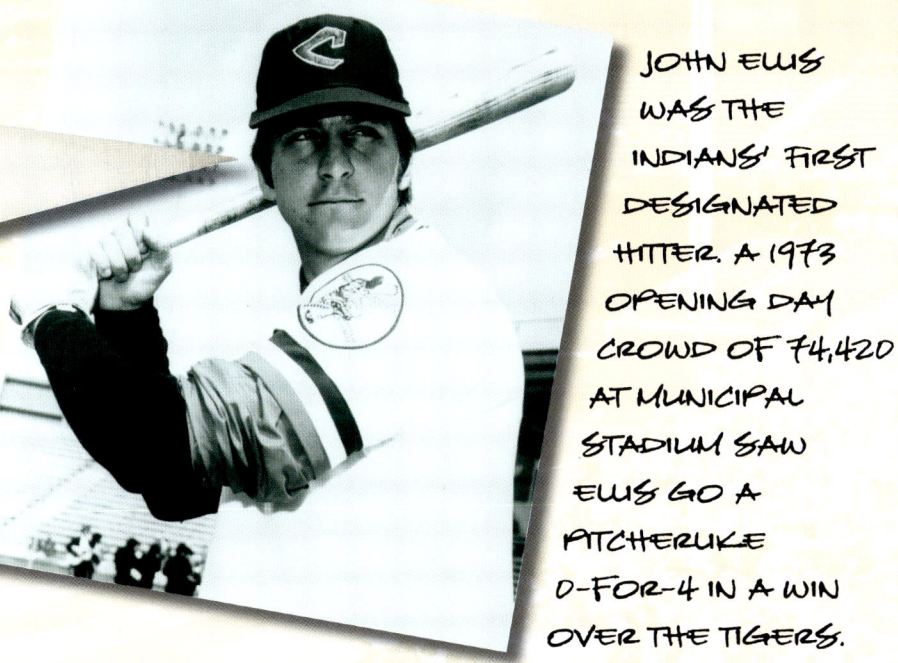

MANY EXPECTED FRANK ROBINSON TO ONE DAY MANAGE IN THE MAJORS, BUT NEW YORK SCRIBE DICK YOUNG HAD A PREMATURE SCOOP IN 1971 WHEN HE TABBED ROBINSON AS THE TRIBE'S NEXT SKIPPER.

Spit and Polish

Indians GM Phil Seghi predicted that Gaylord Perry, despite being four years older than Sam McDowell, would still be pitching long after McDowell was in a rocking chair. This time, Seghi was actually right.

Before the 1972 season, Cleveland traded McDowell, 29, to the San Francisco Giants for the 33-year-old Perry and shortstop Frank Duffy. McDowell drank his way out of baseball by 1975, after winning just 11 games in San Francisco. Perry won 16 games by the 1972 All-Star break. At season's end, he captured the Cy Young Award with 24 wins—one-third of the team's victory total.

Perry's prepitch gyrations—tugging his cap, wiping his brow, and pulling his shirt—fueled suspicions that there was more than leather on the baseballs he pitched. In his 1974 book *Me and the Spitter*, Perry admitted to occasionally tossing a spitball in the past. Perry used his confession as a psychological tool against hitters, leaving them to wonder: Does he, or doesn't he?

Umpires never caught him in the act during his time in Cleveland, although he was nabbed later in his career while playing for Seattle. Indians fans didn't care how Perry won. He was Gaylord the Great. Perry appeared unbeatable for much of the 1974 season, rattling off 15 consecutive wins before losing a one-run, 10-inning game in Oakland. He won 64 games in his first three seasons for the Indians.

Perry's last year in Cleveland would come after much bickering with new manager Frank Robinson. Perry demanded to be paid $1 more than Robinson, a move that hastened Perry's trade to Texas. In exchange, the cash-strapped Indians received $100,000 and three pitchers.

Perry was far from finished. He won another Cy Young in 1978 while with San Diego before winding down his Hall of Fame career in 1983. He ended up with 314 wins and uniforms from eight different teams.

He may have thrown a spitter or two during his time in Cleveland, but Gaylord Perry was far from washed up. He would win another 127 games and another Cy Young Award after the Indians traded him in 1975.

Fans of opposing teams, such as these folks in Milwaukee, were certain Perry and his pitches were all wet. He had many chances to win over fans across the country because he played for eight teams.

Ten-Cent Beers and Five-Cent Heads

On June 4, 1974, the perfect storm bore down on Cleveland Municipal Stadium. The Indians had a frustrated fan base, it was a warm June night, a new rival was in town, and beer was sold for a dime a cup—no limits. The swell that exploded was Ten-Cent Beer Night.

With attendance plummeting, Indians brass was looking for a hook to snare more than the typical 8,000 diehards. But Clevelanders were in a funk from more than bad baseball. Memories of Vietnam, the nearby Kent State shootings, the Hough riots, and general civil unrest still lingered. Jobs dried up, and residents moved out of the city.

Stroh's beer and Texas Rangers manager Billy Martin provided a distraction to 25,000 people in Cleveland Municipal Stadium that night.

This evening's mood was cast just six days earlier when the teams met in Texas and the Rangers held their own cheap-beer promotion. The teams brawled on the field, and Texas fans dumped their suds on Tribe players. Cleveland media promoted the rematch as if it were the showdown at the OK Corral.

"Come out to Beer Night and stick it in Billy Martin's ear!" Indians radio announcer Joe Tait shouted over the airwaves.

The crowd showed up raring to party. Exploding M-80 firecrackers thundered in the upper reaches of the cavernous stadium. A bushy-haired man tussled with a beer vendor. A busty woman stood in the Indians on-deck circle and flashed the crowd to strip-bar hoots of approval. A streaker slid cleanly into second base.

In the ninth, with the Indians rallying to tie the score, fans ran onto the field and charged after Texas right fielder Jeff Burroughs, trying to grab his cap and glove. Martin grabbed a bat and headed out to fend off the savages. Indians Manager Ken Aspromonte urged his team to do the same.

Umpire Nestor Chylak forfeited the game to the Rangers.

Tait summed up the scene from his play-by-play booth: "Mob rule has taken over."

Of the 25,000 in attendance and the dozens who leaped onto the field, just nine people were arrested in the wake of the Ten-Cent Beer Night riot. Seven people were hospitalized as Cleveland police were called in to help the outnumbered security guards disperse the crowd.

Ten-cent cups of reduced-alcohol Stroh's beer were bought six at a time by fans more interested in cheap suds than the Indians' game against the Rangers.

Cleveland Makes History—Again

Frank Robinson dug into the mud next to home plate, surrounded by 56,000 fans and frosty air as another Cleveland winter refused to surrender to spring. It was April 8, 1975, and a mediocre Indians club was making baseball history. All eyes were on Robinson as he debuted as Cleveland's player-manager and Major League Baseball's first African American manager.

Batting himself second as the team's designated hitter, Robinson quickly found himself in a two-strike hole, but the veteran clutch hitter was no stranger to adversity. A hanging slider eventually provided the impetus for one of the most dramatic and memorable events in Indians history: Robinson launched New York Yankees pitcher George "Doc" Medich's pitch over the left-center field fence. The pressure-packed home run helped the Tribe win 5–3.

"Right now I feel better than I have after anything I've done in baseball," Robinson told reporters afterward. "I floated around the bases."

The feeling didn't last long. After all, Cleveland was the graveyard of managers, white *or* black.

Robinson was a leader throughout his career, which began in Cincinnati and continued in Baltimore, Los Angeles, Anaheim, and finally Cleveland, where he landed as a late-season pickup in 1974. Whispers around the majors were that he was a manager-in-waiting and Robinson, who had skippered winter league teams in the off-season, never denied his desire to become the Jackie Robinson of managers. He would get his chance after the Tribe fired manager Ken Aspromonte after the 1974 season and called on Robby to lead the team.

There would be little honeymooning in Cleveland. Veteran pitcher Gaylord Perry—and to a lesser extent his teammate and brother, Jim—didn't take to Robby's hard-charging

Frank Robinson may have been wondering if coming to Cleveland was a wise move. Saddled with poor attendance and a weak minor-league system, the Indians were in the midst of a four-decade drought when he agreed to manage the club.

Opening Day in 1975 marked the first time in the major leagues that an African American manager presented a lineup card to the home plate ump. A throng of cameras followed Frank Robinson's every move, including his home run that afternoon as the team's designated hitter.

leadership. Gaylord Perry, the team's dominant pitcher and top box-office draw, demanded more money than Robinson was getting. He also objected to Robby's demanding spring training regimen. By June 13, 1975, both Perrys had been traded away, leaving no doubt in the clubhouse as to who was in charge.

Despite the promise shown by a trio of rookies—Rick Manning, Duane Kuiper, and Dennis Eckersley—Robinson's Indians didn't challenge in the American League East. He did, however, make some headway as the team finished 79–80, a slight improvement on 1974's 77–85 record. The Indians finished 81–78 in 1976 giving them their first winning record since 1968. Age and injuries were affecting Robinson's hitting, however. After batting .237 in 49 games in 1975 and .224 in 36 games in 1976, Robby retired as a player.

What Robinson couldn't retire were the continued rumblings from older Indians veterans. Rico Carty, a popular Indian called "The Big Mon," blasted Robinson's leadership skills at a fan club awards luncheon in April 1977. Seated nearby were Robinson, club president Ted Bonda, and general manager Phil Seghi. Bonda fired Robinson two months later, with the Indians hovering around the .500 mark. He finished with a 186–189 record as Cleveland's manager and went on to skipper in San Francisco, Baltimore, and Montreal/Washington, D.C.

The Player Who Couldn't Care Less

He could play nearly every position, none exceptionally well or poorly, and he wasn't a great or an awful hitter. So why do Indians fans fondly remember John Lowenstein? He couldn't care less. That's why his fans affectionately dubbed themselves the Apathy Club, and Lowenstein liked them best when the stadium was empty.

"It's the apathy fan club," Steiner once said. "By not being here, there are 80,000 fans showing their support."

In a statistical quirk, he hit .242 three times in four seasons in Cleveland. He also played every position except pitcher and catcher. The Tribe once traded him to Toronto, in December 1976, only to reacquire him three months later. He later blossomed as a platoon outfielder in Baltimore, where he hit 24 home runs in 1982 and played in two World Series.

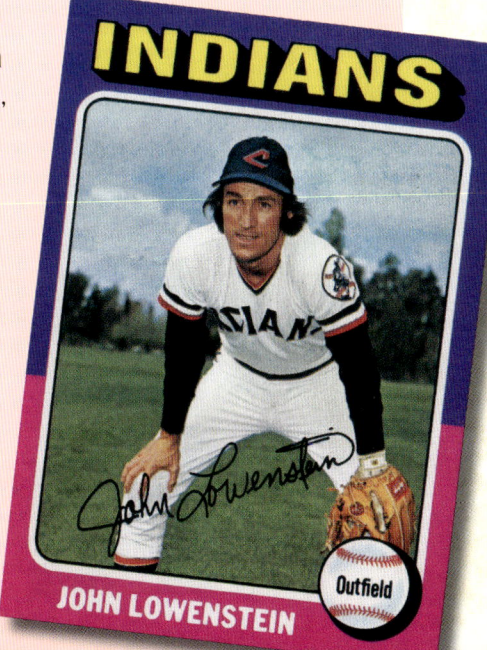

Andre the Giant

He brought thunder to an otherwise languid Indians lineup and dignity to a rather feral and rambunctious clubhouse. Andre Thornton was a sort of baseball anomaly during his 10 seasons in Cleveland. No tobacco, booze, or drugs—only a bat and an intense faith in God that was tested to its limits by death and injury.

Thornton came to Cleveland after the 1976 season in a lopsided trade with Montreal for pitcher Jackie Brown. Nicknamed "Thunder" for his power-hitting prowess, the first baseman and designated hitter led the Indians in home runs seven times. He was a two-time All-Star and a 1984 Silver Slugger winner as a designated hitter, delivering 33 dingers and 99 RBI for the Tribe.

Thornton smacked 214 home runs as an Indian, which ranked fourth in the team record book when he retired in 1987. But it was Thornton's inner strength that carried him in October 1977, when a car crash killed his wife, Gertrude, and 3-year-old daughter, Theresa. He and his son, Andy, were injured.

"I had to remember that tragedy was not unique to Andre Thornton, we all go through it," he said later. "I knew I had no strength, but I also knew that the Lord did, so I didn't need anything else."

Thornton came back in the 1978 season, blasting 33 homers and knocking in 105 runs. He won the 1979 Roberto Clemente Award for his sportsmanship and community work. His fighting spirit won him the 1982 Hutch Award as he recovered from knee surgery to hit 32 home runs and collect a career-high 116 RBI. He also earned *The Sporting News* Comeback Player of the Year Award in 1982.

Even in retirement, Thunder continues his community work in Cleveland, volunteering his time for various charities and groups, many of which focus on education.

In an Indians lineup lacking punch, Andre Thornton delivered. Five times he topped 25 home runs while overcoming his own personal tragedy and injuries. He was named the team's Man of the Year in 1978 and 1982.

From Super Joe to Average Joe

Times were tough, and Cleveland needed a guy who could fix his own broken nose with pliers and who could open a beer bottle with his eye socket before sucking the suds through his nostril. "Super Joe" Charboneau was that man, albeit for just one memorable season in 1980.

No one knew if Charboneau's legend outran reality. Pulling his own tooth, surviving an ink pen stabbing in Mexico, and closing wounds with a needle and thread were great stories. Reporters ate up Super Joe's every word, and fans cheered his every move and wacky-color hair.

"Every city I went to, the stories got bigger and bigger and even different," he marveled to sportswriter Russell Schneider.

The Indians picked up Charboneau from Philadelphia for the low price of floundering pitcher Cardell Camper. After Charboneau lit up minor-league pitching in 1979, star-starved Cleveland provided his next stage. An injury to Andre Thornton put Super Joe in the Tribe's starting lineup in left field (left fielder Mike Hargrove moved from left to first to replace Thornton). Charboneau debuted on Opening Day in Anaheim, California, hitting his first homer in his first game as an Indian. He hit two more for 61,753 fans at the Tribe's home opener a week later.

Charboneau's legend only grew during a trip to grand old Yankee Stadium, where he hit a monstrous blast into the third deck. The pop-culture phenomenon was now in full flurry. A song, "Go Joe Charboneau," and a book, *Super Joe: The Life and Legend of Joe Charboneau*, capitalized on the 25-year-old's sudden popularity.

At season's end, Charboneau captured the AL Rookie of the Year Award, batting .289 with 23 home runs and 87 RBI. For whatever reason—a back injury or smarter pitchers—the phenom ended up a one-year wonder. Charboneau managed just six homers in 70 games over the next two seasons. Super Joe played his last game on June 1, 1982.

The wild stories "Super Joe" Charboneau brought with him to Cleveland were boundless. His handiwork with self-administered dentistry was just one of them. Unfortunately, he could do nothing for the back injury he suffered in 1981.

For one memorable summer in 1980, Charboneau became a Cleveland icon. After hitting .210 and .214 the next two seasons, he was back in the minors and on his way to the semipro sandlots as his flaming star fizzled.

Perfecto!

For one night, Len Barker was perfect. He commanded every pitch—his fastball buzzed and danced, and his curve dipped and dashed like never before. Twenty-seven Toronto Blue Jays took their hacks against Barker at Municipal Stadium on May 15, 1981. All 27 failed to reach base against "Large Lenny."

"I was in the zone, pitching-wise," Barker recalled. "They weren't even hitting the ball after the fourth inning."

Although tens of thousands of Indians fans claim to have been in the stands for Barker's perfect game, the official attendance that blustery night was only 7,290. More watched the game on television station WUAB or listened on radio station WWWE. Some rushed to the ballpark in time to see center fielder Rick Manning squeeze the 27th out of Cleveland's perfect 3–0 victory.

The 6'5" Barker was considered a rising star who won 19 games in 1980 while fanning an AL-best 187 batters. That perfect night against Toronto, there were few bang-bang plays at first, no controversial calls, and Barker required only marginal defensive heroics.

As Ernie Whitt's harmless fly ball nestled in Manning's leather, a celebration unseen since 1948 was unleashed at Municipal Stadium. Fans and reporters mauled the 25-year-old Barker, who had tossed just the eighth perfect game of the modern era (post-1900). Only 14 official perfect games were pitched in the 20th century.

Barker went on to pitch two more memorable perfect innings that season at Municipal Stadium. He did it in front of 72,086 fans in his only All-Star Game appearance.

Seventy-four of the 103 pitches Len Barker tossed in his perfect game against the Toronto Blue Jays were strikes. Although he was known as a power pitcher with a 96-mph fastball, it was his curveball that ruled the chilly night. All 11 of his strikeouts came after the third inning, and all were on fruitless swings.

Fogged In

Only in Cleveland. That's the feeling you get when even Mother Nature turns against the Indians. Case in point: a thick fog that may have cost the Tribe a game against the Red Sox on May 27, 1986.

The Indians were trailing 2–0 with two on in the sixth inning. Pat Tabler was batting when the pea soup drifted off Lake Erie and settled over Municipal Stadium.

Boston players complained they couldn't see, so Indians coach Bobby Bonds hit a few fungoes to test the conditions. Umpires delayed the game for 90 minutes before calling it quits, giving Boston the win.

Afterward, Boston pitcher Dennis "Oil Can" Boyd remarked, "What do you expect when they build a ballpark on the ocean?"

Baseball Resurrected in Cleveland

They weren't the best of times in Cleveland. In 1981, the city was broke and nationally embarrassed as it continued its emergence from financial default. Public school desegregation was in full swing, revealing deep racial tension. A once-vibrant downtown where thousands had celebrated a World Series championship had grown increasingly barren and desolate.

Sports offered no relief. In January, Browns fans watched in horror as Red Right 88, Brian Sipe's would-be game-winning touchdown pass, turned into a last-minute Oakland Raider interception and the first of many playoff heartbreaks. Ted Stepien, the quirky owner of the Cavaliers, gutted the basketball franchise with moves that further humiliated Cleveland.

And baseball? Well, thanks to ugly conflicts between the players and owners (mostly over the new concept of free agency), the players walked off the job on June 12. The strike delayed the one sporting event Clevelanders could embrace: the All-Star Game, which was scheduled for July 14 at Municipal Stadium.

The strike was settled 50 days later on July 31. As a warm-up to an abbreviated and odd split-season schedule, the midsummer classic would be baseball's comeback.

An All-Star Game–record 72,086 fans came out on August 9 to welcome baseball back. To the chagrin of Indians fans, Len Barker did not get the start, despite his perfect game in May. Instead, Detroit's Jack Morris got the nod. Joining Barker on the team was Indians catcher Bo Diaz.

Reggie Jackson, Rod Carew, and George Brett were among the AL's star attractions. Rookie star Fernando Valenzuela started for an NL squad that featured Nolan Ryan, Pete Rose, Mike Schmidt, and game MVP Gary Carter. The game was actually a thriller, as the NL came from behind to win 5–4. Baseball was back, but scars would remain.

Vice President and former Yale first baseman George Bush drew the assignment of tossing out the ceremonial first pitch of the 1981 All-Star Game. His appearance came five months after an assassination attempt on President Ronald Reagan.

Captains of the Titanic

Former Indians owner Alva Bradley once said he never fired a manager in his 20 years as owner—he left that dirty work to the fans. Cleveland field generals have been brave souls, venturing into the Indians dugout, past the ghosts of fallen pilots, and into the renowned graveyard of managers. Nine men took the Cleveland challenge from 1977 to 1991. None stood a chance.

Jeff Torborg replaced Frank Robinson midway through the 1977 campaign. His inexperience and lack of talented players (there's a theme here) fueled his demise in 1979 after his teams went 157–201. Longtime coach Dave Garcia was turning 60 when he replaced Torborg in midseason. Garcia's Indians went 38–28 over the last 66 games. Grand predictions followed, but so did failure.

"Considering what I have to work with," he told reporters in 1982, "I think I have done my best job ever as a manager." The Indians released Garcia at season's end.

Enter Mike Ferraro, formerly a hard-nosed manager in the New York Yankees farm system. Indians president Gabe Paul, who had returned to Cleveland after a stint as Yankees president and GM, was a fan—for 100 games. Kidney cancer took its toll on Ferraro, and Paul fired him after a 40–60 start. Hell-raiser Pat Corrales took over and survived 102 losses in 1985, but got Cleveland over .500 in 1986. However, he couldn't outlast a 31–56 start in 1987. In all, Corrales was 280–355 with the Tribe.

Likable Doc Edwards (173–207) took over and managed the Tribe until 19 games remained in 1989. Future GM John Hart stomached the final contests, going 8–11. Veteran skipper John McNamara (102–137) followed, leading Cleveland to a fourth-place finish in 1990, but he couldn't finish 1991. That season saw the Indians lose 105 games, but Johnny Mac was responsible for only half.

Mike Hargrove endured the rest of 1991, going 32–53, but brighter days were ahead as Cleveland started to catch up with the rest of baseball.

Dave Garcia was one of the few Indians managers who actually won more games than he lost. After taking over for Jeff Torborg midway through the 1979 season, the soft-spoken Garcia's record in three-plus years with the Indians was 247-244.

Pat Corrales was hot-tempered and feisty, but he was no match for Oakland pitcher Dave Stewart, who decked the Tribe skipper during a memorable brawl in 1986. His teams had a forgettable .441 winning percentage.

One-Man Wrecking Crew

It was the Chicago Cubs, not the Indians, who insisted Joe Carter be part of the trade that sent Rick Sutcliffe to Chicago in 1984. And for most of his six seasons in Cleveland, Carter led the Indians offense.

Cleveland had never seen the likes of Joe Carter. Combining devastating power with dashing speed, he was the first Indian to smack more than 100 home runs and swipe more than 100 bases. He did it over six seasons at Municipal Stadium where, as *Sports Illustrated* pointed out, "he was considered as much a part of Cleveland as the steel plants."

Carter played like an ordinary Joe when he came to the Indians with outfielder Mel Hall from the Cubs in the 1984 deal that sent pitcher Rick Sutcliffe to Chicago. While Sutcliffe captured the 1984 NL Cy Young Award, Carter and Hall looked mediocre and had fans feeling as though the Indians were on the wrong end of another one-sided deal.

However, from 1986 through 1989, Carter proved anything but ordinary. The outfielder-first baseman averaged 31 home runs, 108 RBI, and 25 stolen bases. He had 121 RBI in 1986 to top the AL, making Carter the first Indian to do so since Rocky Colavito in 1965.

His bat was one of the reasons *Sports Illustrated* predicted an Indians pennant in 1987. Carter had a fine season, hitting 32 homers, driving in 106 runs, and stealing 31 bases, becoming the first Indian member of the 30–30 club. But World Series dreams went up in smoke as the team lost 101 games.

Carter turned down a long-term contract offer because he was tired of the losing, the decaying stadium, and the cash-strapped team. It was no secret he would become a free agent in 1990.

Clevelanders, who don't take rejection lightly, showered Carter with boos.

"So, of course, I had to be superhuman," he said.

Instead of losing Carter, the Indians traded him to the San Diego Padres. The Tribe received Minor League Player of the Year Sandy Alomar, Jr.; outfielder Chris James; and a prospect named Carlos Baerga.

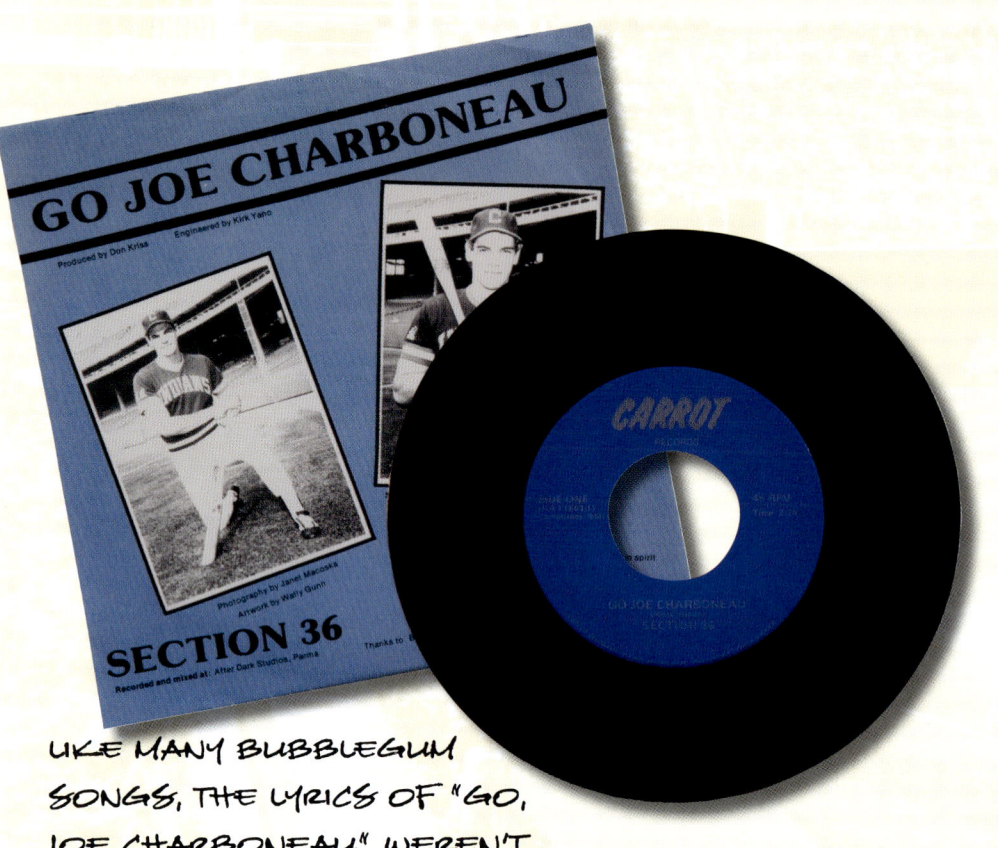

LIKE MANY BUBBLEGUM SONGS, THE LYRICS OF "GO, JOE CHARBONEAU" WEREN'T REMARKABLE OR MEMORABLE, BUT THE SONG DOES OWN A PLACE IN CLEVELAND POP-CULTURE HISTORY.

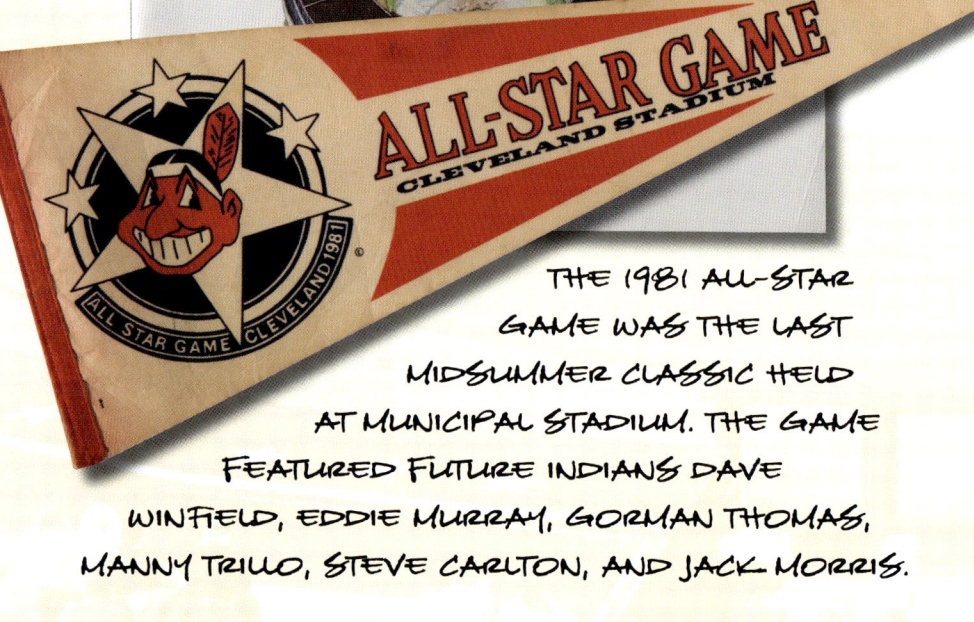

LEN BARKER REMAINS A LOCAL FAVORITE IN CLEVELAND, WHERE HE LIVES AND OPERATES HIS OWN COMPANY, PERFECT PITCH CONSTRUCTION.

THE 1981 ALL-STAR GAME WAS THE LAST MIDSUMMER CLASSIC HELD AT MUNICIPAL STADIUM. THE GAME FEATURED FUTURE INDIANS DAVE WINFIELD, EDDIE MURRAY, GORMAN THOMAS, MANNY TRILLO, STEVE CARLTON, AND JACK MORRIS.

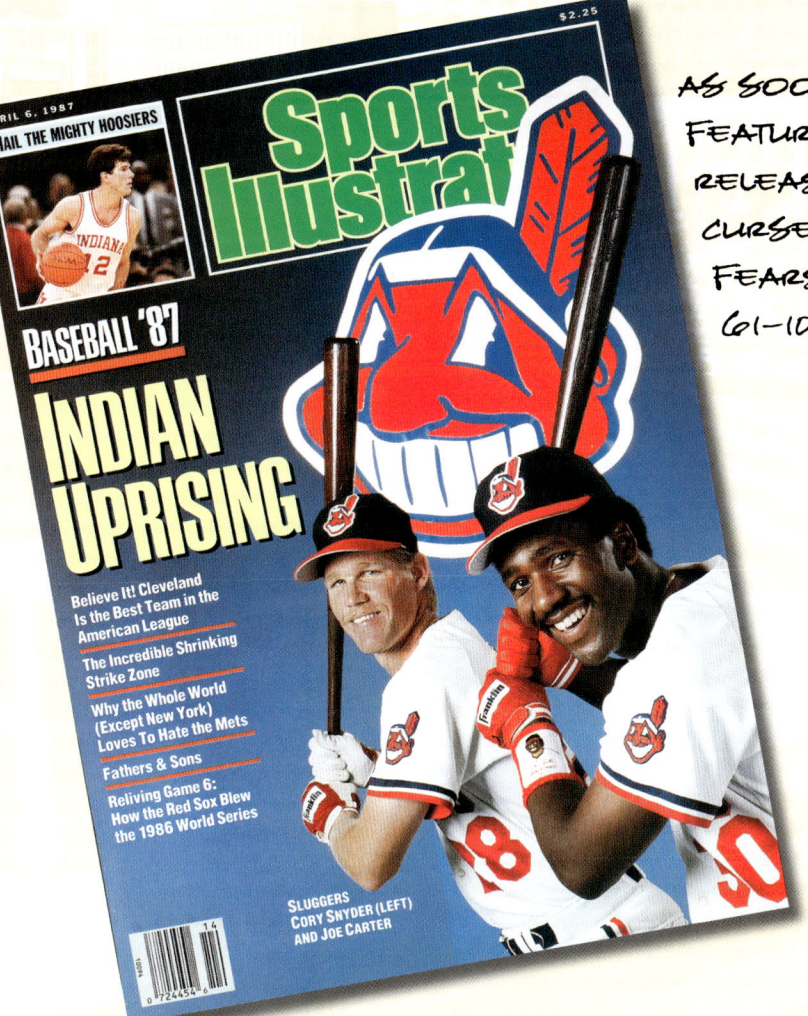

As soon as the Sports Illustrated cover featuring Cory Snyder and Joe Carter was released before opening day 1987, fans cursed the dreaded SI cover jinx. Their fears were realized when the Indians went 61-101.

For the record, it was Indians infielder Mark Lewis who struck out swinging on a Jose DeLeon pitch, thus ending the team's tenure at Municipal Stadium. Pinch runner Manny Ramirez was stranded at second base.

There was a time when only in the movies could Indians fans see a winner wearing a Cleveland uniform. "Wild Thing" Rick Vaughn and his fictional teammates tasted elusive victory in Major League. Local fans complained because most of the action was filmed in Milwaukee.

Spring Training Tragedy

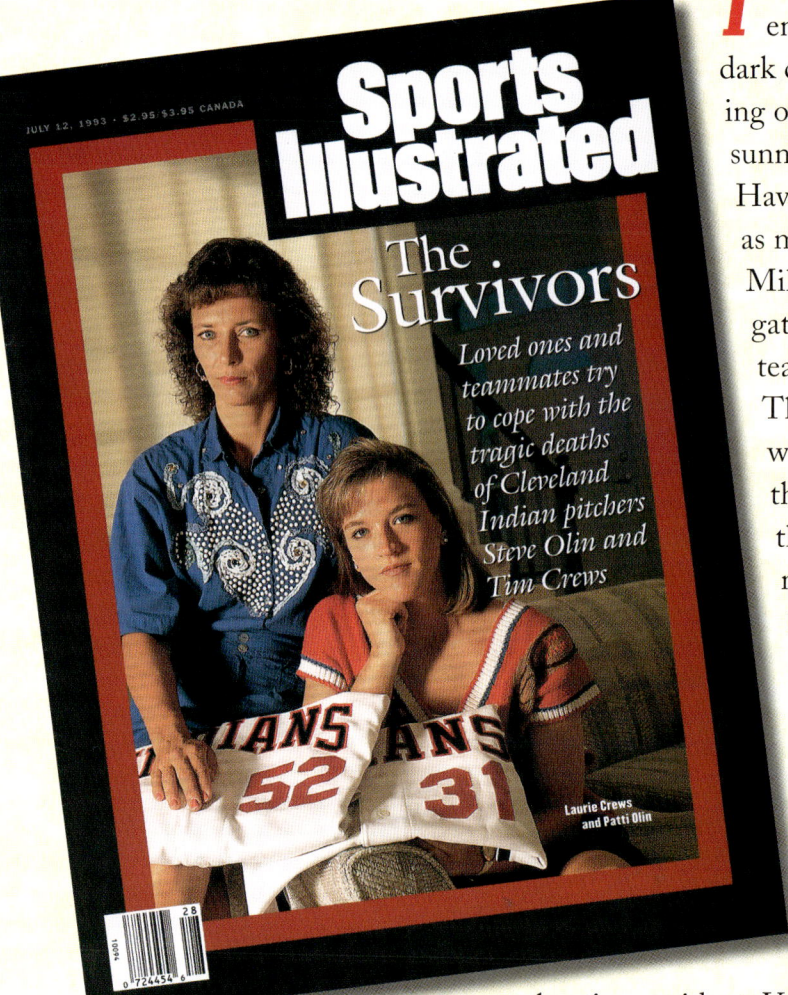

There was an enormous dark cloud hanging over usually sunny Winter Haven, Florida, as manager Mike Hargrove gathered his team in a circle. The Indians were missing three players that spring morning in 1993. The night before, promising closer Steve Olin and reliever Tim Crews had died in a boating accident. Veteran righthander Bob Ojeda had been critically injured.

A spring of hope vanished into a winter of despair for the team and for sudden widows Laurie Crews and Patti Olin.

"We'll get through this," Hargrove said. "We'll get through this because of who we are."

March 22 had been an off-day for Indians players. Crews, a free-agent pickup who was new to the team, invited Indians players and their families for a barbecue at his nearby home on Little Lake Nellie. A day of fun turned into a night of grief when Crews crashed his 18-foot fishing boat into a poorly lighted dock. Alcohol and high speed contributed to the accident. Olin died instantly, Crews the following day. Ojeda suffered a head injury that kept him off the field until August.

In 1992, Olin, then 27, had emerged as the Tribe's closer and picked up 29 saves. Crews, 31 at the time, was signed away from the Los Angeles Dodgers to provide bullpen leadership. Instead, the crash left two widows with three fatherless children each and a young baseball team devastated. No teammate was affected more than pitcher Kevin Wickander, who was Olin's best friend. Wickander mourned the loss to such an extent that he was traded away to Cincinnati that same season.

"When you lose an Olin and a Crews, with a young club, that's a major concern," GM John Hart said. "But no excuses: We're taking the high road. This tragedy is going to bring us closer together."

Support shined on the final Opening Day at Municipal Stadium, where 73,290 paused for a pregame ceremony. Bullpen pitchers donned parts of Olin's and Crews's uniforms. Patti Olin and Laurie Crews received their husbands' jerseys. Indians players wore a patch on their jerseys all season. It was shaped like a baseball and featured Olin's No. 31 near an arrow and Crews's No. 52 near a star.

The Indians kept the jerseys of relievers Steve Olin and Tim Crews hanging in the clubhouse long after the tragic boating accident that claimed the pitchers' lives in 1993.

Goodbye, Muny

More than 2 million fans, the most since the days of Bill Veeck, passed through Municipal Stadium's turnstiles in the summer of 1993 as the Indians prepared to leave for new digs. It wasn't a painful closing. The Indians packed youthful punch. Albert Belle smacked 38 homers, Kenny Lofton stole 70 bases, and second baseman Carlos Baerga hit .321 with 21 homers and 114 RBI.

More than 210,000 came to see them play the White Sox in the final series at the stadium. Tickets were not torn as fans passed the turnstiles. Instead, each was imprinted with a commemorative logo.

On the final day, a throng of former stars returned for the closing ceremony. Mel Harder, who had pitched the first Indians game at Muny in 1932, tossed the ceremonial first pitch. Cleveland native and former Indians co-owner Bob Hope sang "Thanks for the Memories." After the Tribe's 4–0 loss, workers removed home plate and took it to the new baseball palace on Ontario Street.

"While many older Tribe fans have warm memories of Cleveland Stadium, most would admit that the park was like a weird relative," sportswriter Terry Pluto wrote. "You may like and understand him, but there are a lot of good reasons no one else does."

The game itself was almost an afterthought as thousands came on the last day of the 1993 season to say good-bye to Municipal Stadium.

Chief Wahoo may be down, but he's not out. The neon-lighted mascot sign that once rotated above Gate D outside Municipal Stadium is now housed at the Western Reserve Historical Society in Cleveland.

Switch-Hit Swats

History was lost on many inside Municipal Stadium on April 8, 1993. Only those paying close attention immediately realized what switch-hitting second baseman Carlos Baerga did in the bottom of the seventh inning against the Yankees. The right-handed-batting Baerga hit a two-run homer off reliever Steve Howe. Later that same inning, Baerga swung left-handed against reliever Steve Farr and launched a solo shot over the fence. Baerga was the only player ever to hit home runs from both sides of the plate in the same inning, until Mark Bellhorn of the Chicago Cubs matched his feat in 2002.

CHAPTER SIX

Tribe Turnaround 1994–2000

GOOD THINGS ARE worth waiting for, even if the wait is 40 torment-filled years. Not since the 1954 season did Cleveland Indians fans have so much to embrace. For the first time since 1933, the team played in a new ballpark, this one a luxurious gem that was the envy of the major leagues. The Tribe was also decked out in snazzy new uniforms that helped show off this new contender to the rest of the country. The improvements energized a fan base to the point of frenzy: It was finally a good time to root for the Indians again.

Construction of Jacobs Field and its neighbor, now known as Quicken Loans Arena, sparked development on the south side of downtown Cleveland, fostering a renaissance that bolstered the city's economy and its national image.

While some teams shied away from drafting the volatile Albert Belle, the Indians took the powerful outfielder in the second round of the 1987 draft. Belle quickly emerged as one of baseball's most feared sluggers.

As fans drove east over the Lorain-Carnegie Bridge in 1994, Jacobs Field rose out of the old Central Market neighborhood, glistening like a diamond in the rough. Opening Day that year ushered in a new beginning for the city, its team, and its fans.

101

Cleveland's Crown Jewel

Jacobs Field was briefly called Indians Park in 1994 before Tribe owner Richard Jacobs purchased the stadium's naming rights for $13.9 million over 20 years. Jacobs slapped his name on the stadium just before it opened with an exhibition game against the Pittsburgh Pirates.

All signs pointed to the corner of Ontario and Carnegie, where a city and its baseball team marked a turnaround.

She was simply stunning. For Indians fans who had endured the drab years at Municipal Stadium, Jacobs Field was like a fantasy land. Clean concrete and a yellow-brick façade framed the new grandeur, while 19 toothbrush-shape light towers reached toward the sky. The more than 41,000 sparkling seats (later expanded to more than 43,000) each offered a view of the Cleveland skyline and created an intimacy reminiscent of old League Park.

The smooth clay and sand infield reached out to kiss the lush Kentucky bluegrass that covered the asymmetrical outfield. A miniature Green Monster in left field accommodated standing fans with a plaza. A glass-enclosed restaurant offered fans a meal with a view unmatched anywhere in the city. The wealthy and the corporate set now had 122 luxury suites on three levels to host friends and clients. The playland in a concourse beyond the right field fence entertained the younger crowd. A picnic area in center field offered barbeque delights fresh off the grill. And looking down upon it all was a mammoth scoreboard with "Indians" in illuminated script.

Tickets to the first game at the Jake were hard to come by, but those that were used were respected. Ushers stamped the ducats with an impression, and fans slid them into commemorative frames to fend off stains and bends.

"I think we have the greatest facility for baseball," owner Richard Jacobs said before Opening Day of the 1994 season. And many agreed.

For nearly 40 years, Indians owners, desperate to escape huge, echo-filled Municipal Stadium, pleaded for a new ballpark. Jacobs, who bought the team with his brother, David, in 1986 for $36 million, was finally able to negotiate a deal with the county government. Cuyahoga County voters agreed by a narrow 1.2-percent margin to a tax on alcohol and tobacco to fund the $170 million baseball park and an adjacent arena (now known as Quicken Loans Arena) that cost an additional $161 million. Jacobs paid nearly $14 million to name the baseball park after himself.

The facilities weren't just places to play games—they were vessels of hope for a decaying downtown. Eager Indians fans gobbled up more than 2 million tickets before the first ball was thrown. When ushers finally rolled back the Jake's iron gates on April 4, 1994, immediate comparisons were drawn to Camden Yards in Baltimore, the first of baseball's retro complexes. More than 41,000 fans soaked it in as the park was showered with praise from across the country. President Bill Clinton donned an Indians jacket to ward off the typical April chill and tossed the ceremonial first pitch.

Dennis Martinez, a free agent signed over the winter, drew the start for the Indians. Randy Johnson pitched for the Seattle Mariners and flirted with a no-hitter through seven innings. The game went into the 11th inning before Indians reserve outfielder Wayne Kirby slapped a single to score Eddie Murray, and the Indians prevailed 4–3. Cleveland definitely had a winner.

Southpaw President Bill Clinton donned an Indians warm-up jacket to toss out the ceremonial first pitch to open Jacobs Field. Governor George Voinovich and Mayor Michael White were also on hand.

Make Room for Eddie

There was a time when a player of Eddie Murray's stature would rather retire than play in Cleveland. It goes to show how a new ballpark and a promising team can attract even the most discerning tastes.

Murray signed as a free agent before the 1994 season. He brought his hunt for 3,000 career hits with him, and he reached the milestone in Minnesota on June 30, 1995. Although Murray joined Pete Rose as the only switch-hitting 3,000-hit club members, he was rather ho-hum about it.

"It was nice," he said. "But 3,000 is just a number."

Murray went on to join Hank Aaron and Willie Mays as the only players with 3,000 hits and 500 home runs before entering the ultimate baseball club: The Hall of Fame.

Surly Slugger

The new Indians walked with a swagger, and no one flaunted it more than Albert Belle, who intimidated teammates just as well as he did opposing pitchers with his ever-present snarl. Belle would hit a career-high .357 in 1994.

As he stormed into the dugout, Albert Belle turned toward the Red Sox bench, flexed his bicep, and pointed at the mound of muscle. He was infuriated over Boston's demand that his bat be checked for cork. That moment in the 1995 playoffs defined the slugger for a nation.

Belle was fiery, strong, and dastardly intimidating, whether chasing pranksters on Halloween or angrily tossing balls at fans or photographers. Belle did not discriminate, imposing his venom on teammates, reporters—even a clubhouse thermostat when he thought it too hot.

But he could club a baseball like few others.

The corking allegations had been floating since "Batgate" a year earlier in Chicago. Umpires had confiscated Belle's bat, but Indians reliever Jason Grimsley crawled through the Comiskey Park ceiling to the umpires' locker room and switched Belle's bat with another. The scheme failed, because the bat Grimsley left behind had first baseman Paul Sorrento's name on it. Legend has it that all of Belle's bats were corked, leaving Grimsley with no choice.

Cork or not, in 1995, Belle clobbered 50 homers and 52 doubles, becoming the only player to hit 50 of each in a season. He'd hit another 48 dingers in 1996 before leaving Cleveland to join the Chicago White Sox as the game's highest-paid player. When he played in Cleveland, fans showed their own venom, dropping paper money and raining boos on him from the plaza in left field.

Señor Save

Kyle Washington's baseball career is noteworthy for one thing: The Indians traded him to Baltimore for Jose Mesa. Even Tribe GM John Hart could not envision his own shrewdness.

From 1992 to 1994, Mesa was a starter in a woeful Indians rotation. The Indians moved him to the bullpen when they signed veteran free agents Jack Morris and Dennis Martinez in 1994. He took hold of the closer job in 1995 and became "Señor Save." Mesa saved a club-record 46 games with a dazzling 1.13 ERA, helping the Indians to their first pennant in 41 years.

The Fast Track to Stardom

It was the eighth inning in Game 6 of the 1995 American League Championship Series. Kenny Lofton, whose two-out single just put the Indians ahead by two, took his lead at second base. As Lofton danced, Mariners pitcher Randy Johnson delivered a sizzler that scooted past his catcher. Lofton wasn't content just taking third. He dashed onward toward home plate using sprinter's speed, easily beating the throw to a stunned Johnson.

Cleveland was on its way to the World Series, and that was Lofton at his finest.

"At this level of play, you can't rely on other teams' mistakes," Lofton once said. "You've got to make things happen."

Lofton's speed from the left side of the plate and his line-drive batting stroke made him a consistent .300 batter and the consummate leadoff hitter. As a baserunner, he rewrote Indians stolen base records. As a center fielder, he was just as peerless, whether tracking down deep fly balls or scaling fences to turn home runs into outs. He captured four consecutive Gold Glove Awards from 1993 to 1996.

Lofton was another of John Hart's finds. The former sixth man on the University of Arizona's 1988 Final Four basketball team, Lofton was toiling in the Houston Astros minor-league system in 1991. Most scouts didn't see stardom—they saw a basketball player in the batter's box.

Hart saw great potential in Lofton's raw speed. For the price of one minor-league catcher and a journeyman pitcher, Lofton came to Cleveland in 1992. A city and a player struck gold. Lofton hit .285 his first season, while stealing 66 bases to set both club and AL rookie records. But that was only the beginning. His 452 career steals in Cleveland are a team record, and he hit .299 over 17 seasons playing with 11 teams.

Kenny Lofton played for 11 different teams in his 17-year career, but his best seasons came during three different stints with the Indians. He parlayed his frequent travels late in his career into a comical TV commercial for a shipping company.

When it came to outfield defense, Kenny Lofton was one of the best. With his speed to the power alleys, he turned surefire doubles or triples into outs. With his leaping ability, he turned home runs into fly-outs in the scorebook.

Pennant Fever: An Epidemic Returns

Tony Peña's game-winning, 13th-inning home run against Boston in the 1995 ALDS came at around 1 A.M. The win was Cleveland's first in the postseason since 1948. But while Drew Carey cheered from his loge, half of Jacobs Field had emptied on this weekday night.

Forget Bill Veeck's 1948 Indians team and the 111-win squad of 1954. When it comes to domination, the 1995 Indians were Cleveland's best ever.

The Tribe went 100-44 in 1995 (a season shortened by the 1994–95 strike) and won the Central Division by an astounding 30 games. No AL team scored more runs, hit more home runs, or stole more bases. No pitching staff gave up fewer earned runs. Six players were All-Stars, and two won Gold Gloves.

Cleveland fans set their own record as 2.8 million passed through Jacobs Field turnstiles, topping the attendance mark set in 1948 at Municipal Stadium. From June 12 on, every game was sold out—52 straight by season's end.

The Indians swept 12 series, prompting a ban on fans bringing brooms to the Jake. Time after time, the Indians overcame deficits, usually in awe-inspiring fashion. They won 27 games in their final at-bat, including 17 in the final inning at Jacobs Field.

"It's almost like it's meant to be," Oakland reliever Dennis Eckersley said after a stunning 12th-inning loss to the Tribe.

By September 8, the Indians celebrated the Central Division title—the team's first clinch in 41 years. Newspapers splashed the news with imposing front-page headlines usually reserved for natural disasters or wars. Television stations devoted nearly their entire 30-minute newscasts to the Indians, as their reporters donned Tribe gear as if they were cheerleaders.

October baseball was returning to Cleveland. When Game 1 of the AL Division Series opened at the Jake, the Indians were facing the Boston Red Sox and long-time nemesis Roger Clemens. The magic that followed the Indians all summer blossomed with two outs in the 13th inning, when backup catcher Tony Peña launched a homer into the left-field bleachers for a 5–4 win. The heroics set the stage for a three-game sweep.

Despite the Tribe's superior record, a rotating playoff format forced the Indians to open the best-of-seven AL Championship Series in Seattle's Kingdome. A no-name rookie, Bob Wolcott, helped hand the Indians a 3–2 loss. After a 5–2 Indians victory in Game 2, the series moved to Cleveland. Another sell-out crowd saw Seattle's Jay Buhner hit an 11th-inning homer that won the game 5–2. Seattle, however, would not win another game. The Tribe crushed the Mariners 7–0 in Game 4 and squeaked by 3–2 in Game 5. Dennis Martinez tossed a masterpiece in Game 6 back at the Kingdome as Cleveland won the pennant with a 4–0 victory.

The World Series that awaited in Atlanta pitted Cleveland's fearsome lineup against baseball's best pitching staff, which featured Greg Maddux, John Smoltz, and Tom Glavine. The first three games were one-run affairs, with the Indians winning only Game 3 at Jacobs Field. Atlanta's Steve Avery stymied the Cleveland bats in Game 4 as the Braves won 5–2 and took a commanding 3–1 lead in the Series.

Game 5 in Cleveland was another close one, with the Indians winning 5–4 behind Orel Hershiser. Indians fans clung to hope as Martinez prepared for Game 6. Unfortunately, this wasn't the year—the Tribe's bats melted in Hotlanta as Glavine and Mark Wohlers combined on a one-hit shutout. David Justice's solo home run tallied the game's only score as the Braves won the game, 1–0, and the Series, 4–2. Cleveland had regained the championship thirst, but the quenching would have to wait.

In 1954, when the Indians last won more than 100 games, Sohio was selling gas for less than a quarter a gallon, a gallon of milk at Lawson's was less than a dollar, and a T-bone from Pick-n-Pay was about 95 cents a pound. Forty-one years would pass before Tribe fans saw triple-digit wins again.

The no-crying-in-baseball rule was suspended in Cleveland, for fans and players alike, including young reliever Julian Tavarez. He shed a few tears following the Indians' Game 6 loss to the Braves in the 1995 World Series.

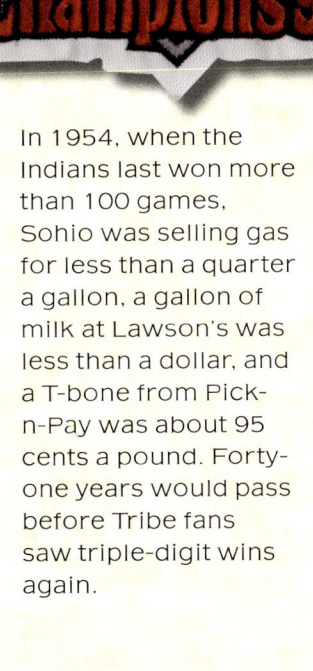

107

WHEN HE CAME TO CLEVELAND, HE WAS JOEY BELLE. BUT AFTER FACING HIS ALCOHOLISM, HE CALLED A PRESS CONFERENCE AND ANNOUNCED HE PREFERRED HIS GIVEN NAME OF ALBERT. GETTING BELLE'S AUTOGRAPH DEPENDED ON THE TEMPERAMENTAL SLUGGER'S MOOD.

CAUGHT UP IN MEMORABILIA FRENZY, INDIANS FANS LINED UP TO BUY PROGRAMS FOR THE FIRST GAME AT JACOBS FIELD. SOME BOUGHT TWO: ONE TO LOOK AT AND ONE TO PRESERVE.

STEPPING OUT OF MUNICIPAL STADIUM AND INTO JACOBS FIELD WAS LIKE DOROTHY LANDING IN OZ. THE ONLY DIFFERENCE WAS THAT DOROTHY WOULD HAVE WANTED TO STAY AT THE JAKE.

CLEVELAND-AREA MCDONALD'S RESTAURANTS CASHED IN ON THE INDIANS' POPULARITY WITH THESE COMMEMORATIVE BASEBALLS. THE PROMOTION TURNED OUT TO BE A TASTY SELL.

IT'S ANOTHER OF THOSE "WHAT IFS" IN INDIANS HISTORY. THE 1994 INDIANS WERE HOT ON THE TRAIL OF DIVISION-LEADING CHICAGO WHEN THE PLAYERS STRIKE CANCELLED THE REST OF THE SEASON ON AUGUST 12.

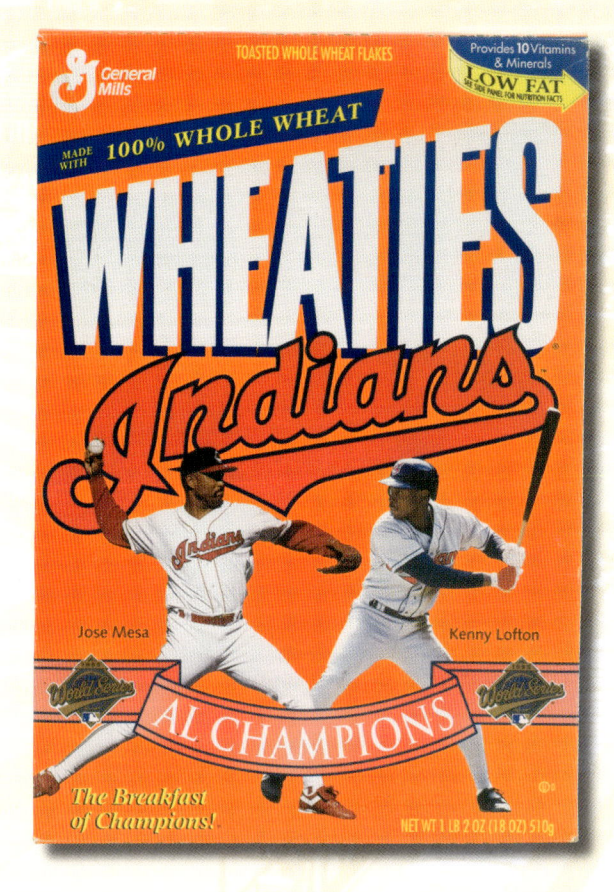

THE 1995 AL CHAMPION INDIANS KNEW THEY HAD ARRIVED IN PRIME TIME WHEN THEY LANDED ON A "BREAKFAST OF CHAMPIONS" BOX.

SERIES SWEEPS BY THE INDIANS AT THE JAKE IN 1995 BECAME SO COMMON THAT FANS CAME ARMED WITH THEIR KITCHEN BROOMS TO MARK EACH OCCASION. THE INDIANS MARKETING DEPARTMENT OFFERED INFLATABLE BROOMS FOR THE EMPTY-HANDED.

THE 1995 INDIANS LINEUP WAS PACKED WITH PUNCH FROM TOP TO BOTTOM. THE TRIBE'S .291 TEAM AVERAGE, 840 RUNS SCORED, 132 STOLEN BASES, .479 SLUGGING PERCENTAGE, AND 207 HOMERS ALL TOPPED THE AMERICAN LEAGUE.

Tribe Pride

Cleveland fans by the thousands packed Public Square on October 30, 1995, for a rally to celebrate the Indians' World Series appearance. Fans still remember shortstop Omar Vizquel's stand-up comedy routine, which helped soothe their disappointment over losing to the Braves two days earlier.

Two generations of Indians fans knew only losing until 1994. For 34 seasons, only six Indian teams won more games than they lost and no team finished higher than third. Scarred by bad trades, a decrepit ballpark, and poor ownership, short-changed fans stayed in touch but steered clear of the ballpark.

Beginning in 1994, Tribe Pride was at a fever pitch. An owner with patience and business sense and a management team committed to developing and retaining talented players had the sleeping giant of Indians fandom abuzz.

Fans waited in winter snow to buy tickets while others jammed phone lines. Indians tickets, of all things, were prizes offered on radio and TV shows. The Indians stopped season tickets sales at 25,000 to allow others a chance to buy tickets to games in the nearly 42,000-seat (later expanded to more than 43,000 seats) park. Those who were shut out paid for tours of the park on days when no games were scheduled.

Companies held Indians days, when employees donned their best Tribe gear. Front yards hosted signs, and office windows were plastered with salutes to the local ballclub. Everyone in Cleveland, it seemed, owned something bearing Chief Wahoo's grin. Suddenly, the Indians were on the map, as their merchandise rivaled Yankees, Cubs, and Dodgers gear in sales.

The Hottest Ticket in Town

Along the mezzanine level at Jacobs Field, next to the retired jersey numbers of Feller, Boudreau, Doby, and others, workers placed the number 455. The three digits pay tribute to Indians fans who did not allow a seat to go unsold for 455 consecutive games.

Attendance records were shattered as more than 3 million fans attended each year from 1996 to 2001. The sellout streak began on June 12, 1995, and continued through the second game of the 2001 season. For five straight seasons, every ticket was sold before Opening Day. Sparkling new Jacobs Field and the resurgent Indians were the main factors, but Art Modell's move of the Browns to Baltimore in 1996 and the mediocrity of the NBA's Cleveland Cavaliers made the Indians essentially the only show in town.

O's No!

There was really no reason for the Indians *not* to return to the World Series in 1996. After dominating the American League in 1995, the Indians added more pop and more pitching to an already-potent roster. Julio Franco, a former Indian who was still a master with the bat, signed to back up at first base and to be a designated hitter. Right-hander Jack McDowell, the AL's Cy Young winner in 1993, inked a deal after a 15-win season with the Yankees.

There were also subtractions. Carlos Baerga, a symbol of the Indians' rebirth, went through a shocking slump and was traded in July to the Mets. He wept to reporters as he left the Indians clubhouse. In return, the Indians received shortstop Jose Vizcaino and second baseman Jeff Kent. A week earlier, veteran Eddie Murray was traded to Baltimore.

The Tribe strutted to a 99-win season and took the Central Division by 14½ games. Pennant fever was once again alive and well in Cleveland. But something happened on the way to the World Series—the Baltimore Orioles.

Thanks to baseball's rotating format, the best-of-five ALDS opened with two games in Camden Yards even though Cleveland had won 11 more games than Baltimore. The O's rocked Charles Nagy in Game 1, 10–4, and did the same to the Indians' usually reliable bullpen in Game 2, as Baltimore won 7–4.

The Indians salvaged Game 3 at the Jake, thanks to a seventh-inning grand slam by Albert Belle. The teams played into the 12th inning of Game 4 when Jose Mesa, pitching his third inning of relief, served up a home run to Roberto Alomar as the Orioles won the game 4–3 and took the series.

Ouch.

Julio Franco, a throwback Indian from the 1980s, returned to the Tribe in 1996 as the team found new frustrations, losing to the underdog Orioles in the ALDS. Franco hit just .133 in the four-game set, about 200 points lower than his season average.

The Indians expected to slug their way back to the World Series in 1996. Instead, the Tribe's mighty lineup hit just .245 in the ALDS, while its normally steady pitchers were battered. Here, Brian Anderson (left) and Albie Lopez feel the pain.

111

Defeat from the Jaws of Victory

Complacency seemed to settle over Jacobs Field. The swagger left with Albert Belle, Dennis Martinez, and Kenny Lofton. The 1997 Indians were different. They won just 86 games, which was still good enough to top the weak Central Division, but few fans expected a World Series trip.

Power-hitting third baseman Matt Williams came in a trade with San Francisco and delivered 32 home runs and 105 RBI. Outfielders David Justice and Marquis Grissom came from Atlanta for Lofton. Justice was sensational—he clubbed 33 dingers and made up for the loss of Belle, who left as a free agent. Sandy Alomar, Jr., had his best year, hitting .324 with 21 homers. He was even named MVP of the All-Star Game, which was played at Jacobs Field. Jim Thome moved from third base to first base and launched 40 homers, a career high for him at the time.

The Tribe had its problems on the mound. Jack McDowell proved he was finished, and Martinez was not re-signed. John Smiley, a former 20-game winner who was acquired from Cincinnati, pitched six games before breaking his arm throwing a pitch. The Indians had to rely on youngsters Chad Ogea, Bartolo Colon, and Jaret Wright.

In the ALDS, the Indians battled the Yankees in dramatic fashion, overcoming a 2–1 series deficit to end the Bronx Bombers' year. Alomar's storybook season continued in Game 4 at the Jake as he smacked a game-tying, fist-pumping homer off New York closer Mariano Rivera in a 3–2 win. Wright continued his Cinderella story, pitching the Indians to a 4–3 win in Game 5.

The ALCS offered more memories, this time against Baltimore. The series was highlighted by Marquis Grissom's controversial steal of home on a missed bunt in a Game 3 victory

It's a scene that remains one of the bitterest moments in Cleveland sports history: Jose Mesa blows the save opportunity in Game 7 of the 1997 World Series. Mesa's days in Cleveland would end the following season, but the dark memory remains ingrained in the hearts of Tribe fans.

Fans treated every World Series game in 1997 as a holiday, taking in the games on TVs that were set up in downtown Cleveland, in local bars, or in backyards. The warmth of an Indian summer turned cold as the championship drought headed toward 50 years.

He may have botched a few calls, and he may have forgotten to give the score here and there, but Indians fans adored pitcher-turned-radio-announcer Herb Score. The voice of the Tribe for generations of long-suffering fans retired after the 1997 Series. His last game behind the mic was the near-miss of Game 7.

and Tony Fernandez's homer in the 11th inning of Game 6 that propelled the Indians to an improbable World Series against the Florida Marlins. The matchup with the Marlins didn't evoke nostalgia among Tribe fans. Heck, the Marlins were only in their fifth season of existence. They were viewed as a team that merely bought its way to the Series, committing $89 million to free agents and a record $7 million for manager Jim Leyland. The Series seemed to come too easy for Marlin fans. There were no years of suffering on South Beach. The Indians deserved this championship, and their wild road to the Series made them appear to be the team of destiny. But Clevelanders would be teased once again.

The teams alternated wins through Game 6 as Ogea matched Bob Lemon's team record, picking up his second Series win. Wright rose to the occasion in Game 7, giving up one run as he pitched into the seventh inning. Fernandez's two-out single gave the Indians a 2–1 lead heading into the ninth. Closer Jose Mesa, a hero from the 1995 team, took the mound. In his book, *Omar!*, written with Bob Dyer, Vizquel recalled looking into Mesa's eyes as the inning started and found "nobody home."

With runners on the corners, Mesa was two outs away from pitching the Indians to their first World Series championship since 1948. Craig Counsell's sacrifice fly, however, scored the tying run. All was lost in the 11th inning as soft-hitting Edgar Renteria singled past Charles Nagy to plate the winning run—a curse continued.

"I couldn't believe it when the Indians beat the Yankees..." columnist Terry Pluto wrote. "Unfortunately, I could believe it when Jose Mesa couldn't hold the lead in the seventh game of the 1997 World Series."

The cost of a Jacobs Field bleacher seat for the 1997 World Series: $30. The cost of a Municipal Stadium reserve seat for the 1954 Series: $7. The cost of the Indians losing both Series: Incalculable.

Magic Man

Over a span of 125 games played in 1997 and 1998, Omar Vizquel committed just one error. At one point, he was errorless in 46 straight postseason games. Legendary Cleveland sportswriter Hal Lebovitz said Vizquel topped Lou Boudreau as the team's best-ever shortstop.

He was flashy and brilliant, whether barehanding groundballs with ease or turning his back to home plate to catch ordinary pop-ups. Indians fans came to love Omar Vizquel. Better yet, they grew to *appreciate* the Gold Gloved shortstop.

He shopped with Clevelanders at the West Side Market and danced with them at clubs around the city. Fans bought his salsa, ice cream, and signature clothing. No Indian smiled more often. No Tribesman ripped more one-liners. As the seasons passed and players moved on, no Indian was more popular.

In a lineup filled with bashers and mashers, Vizquel performed the small feats with grace and beauty, winning nine straight Gold Glove Awards (eight with Cleveland) while complementing the order as the No. 2 hitter.

"He's so good," Mariners outfielder Jay Buhner said. "He's calm, cool, and confident. He's a cocky little [expletive], but damn good."

The Indians acquired Vizquel from Seattle before the 1994 season for Reggie Jefferson and Felix Fermin in another stroke of genius and luck by general manager John Hart. In one of his first games at the Jake, Vizquel stunned fans by committing three errors against the Kansas City Royals. The stand-up guy didn't dodge reporters' questions afterward, and he never played as poorly again.

Vizquel hit .280 or better in six of his seasons in Cleveland and stole 29 or more bases five times. In an era of power-hitting shortstops, Vizquel was a three-time All Star.

Longtime Indians fans contend that Vizquel is the greatest shortstop in Indians history—even better than the popular Lou Boudreau. Others say he's the best defensive shortstop baseball has ever seen, and that includes Hall of Famer Ozzie Smith.

"Five years after he retires, Vizquel should follow Smith to Cooperstown," *News-Herald* Indians beat writer Jim Ingraham wrote.

The Brain Trust

They weren't exactly golf buddies. No, John Hart and Mike Hargrove often had different ideas when it came to running the Indians. That's not surprising because it was Hart's job as general manager to fill the Indians roster, and it was Grover's job to win with them.

Predictably, they were an odd couple.

"A relationship that's smooth sailing all the way is probably not worth having," Hargrove once said.

Hart was Felix Ungar, always tanned and wearing designer sunglasses. He was fit and well-dressed, a yuppie of sorts, with a penchant for detail and motivation. Hargrove, on the other hand, was Oscar Madison, a player's manager with a potbelly. He was a former Indians first baseman, known as the "Human Rain Delay" because of a series of gyrations he went through during every at-bat. As a manager, he wasn't a tyrant or a strategic genius. As long as the Indians were winning, the skipper ran a loose ship.

Despite all the winning, discontent seemed to permeate the relationship between Hart and Hargrove.

"The underlying cause of dissent might well be that Hargrove is as patient as Hart is impatient," wrote Jon Heyman of *The Sporting News*.

Hargrove wasn't Hart's hire. Midway through the 1991 season, club president Hank Peters hired Grover, who had managed in the Indians' farm system. Hart, the protégé of Peters, was named GM by year's end. The shrewd Hart realized the team's limited income in a small market, so he signed young players to long-term deals, forgoing arbitration and delaying free agency.

Although he assembled a lineup full of All-Stars, a stud pitcher always eluded Hart in his trades. Fans bemoaned his dealing of prospects like Brian Giles for reliever Ricardo Rincon; Sean Casey for starter Dave Burba; and Richie Sexson for three pitchers, including reliever Bob Wickman.

After the Indians' quick exit from the playoffs in 1999, Hart fired Hargrove, who had spent 22 years in the Cleveland organization as a player, coach, and manager. Two seasons later, Hart resigned.

Despite their unmatched success, Indians GM John Hart (*right*) was criticized for failing to land a pitching ace, and manager Mike Hargrove was blamed for failing to win a World Series.

NO INDIAN STARTED THE 1997 ALL-STAR GAME AT JACOBS FIELD, BUT RESERVE CATCHER SANDY ALOMAR, JR., TOOK MVP HONORS AFTER HIS TWO-RUN HOMER IN THE SEVENTH INNING PUT THE AL AHEAD FOR GOOD.

DAVID JUSTICE'S HOMER AGAINST THE INDIANS WON THE 1995 WORLD SERIES FOR THE BRAVES. AS AN INDIAN, HE HIT JUST .185 WITH NO HOME RUNS IN THE 1997 SERIES.

BROTHERS SANDY ALOMAR, JR. (CENTER), AND ROBERTO ALOMAR WERE AMONG THE BEST AT THEIR POSITIONS DURING THE 1990S. THEIR FATHER, SANDY ALOMAR, SR., PLAYED 15 SEASONS IN THE MAJORS.

THE 1997 ALCS BETWEEN THE TRIBE AND THE HEAVILY FAVORED ORIOLES RANKS AS ONE OF THE MOST EXCITING POSTSEASON MATCHUPS IN CLEVELAND SPORTS HISTORY.

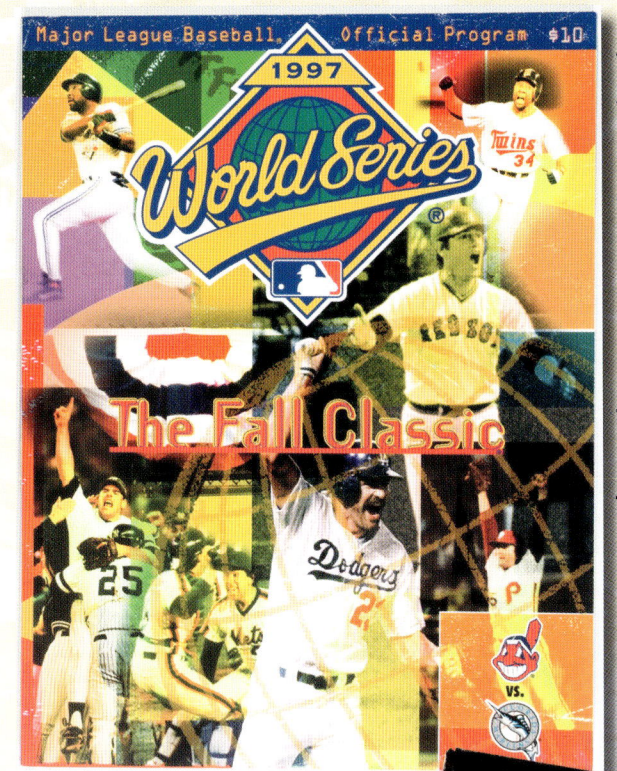

THE INDIANS LOST TWO OF THREE GAMES PLAYED AT THE JAKE IN THE 1997 WORLD SERIES. THEIR ONLY HOME WIN CAME FROM JARET WRIGHT, WHO PITCHED AMID SNOW FLURRIES THAT OPENED GAME 4.

JIM THOME SMACKED FOUR HOME RUNS, AND OMAR VIZQUEL HIT .440 IN THE 1998 ALCS AGAINST THE YANKEES, BUT THE TRIBE COULD NOT HIT NEW YORK SOUTHPAW DAVID WELLS, WHO STRUCK OUT 18 IN TWO WINS.

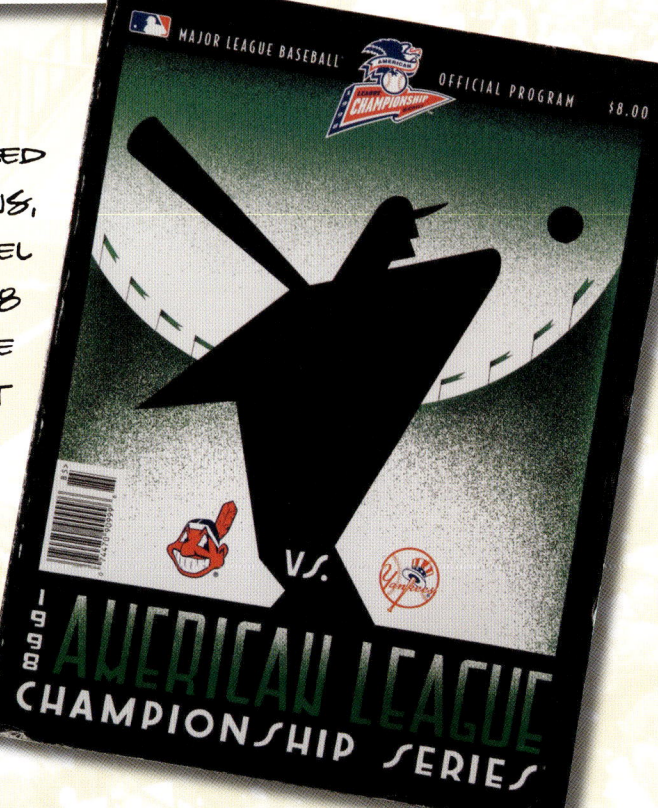

CLEVELAND WAS PRIME-TIME READY AS A NATION TOOK NOTICE OF THE REJUVENATION OF THE INDIANS AND THE CITY.

Still No Cigar

Chad Ogea's success in the 1997 World Series didn't carry over to the 1998 ALCS. He relieved Jaret Wright in Game 1 and served up a homer to Yankees catcher Jorge Posada (*above*). Ogea didn't fare much better in Game 5, and the Yankees went on to win the series.

Two World Series losses in three years kept the Indians hungry. In 1998, the Tribe once again dominated and won the Central Division by nine games. The Indians were still a hitting team, and Manny Ramirez had a monstrous year, pounding 45 homers and collecting 145 RBI. Jim Thome smacked 30 dingers, and Travis Fryman, the team's new third baseman, added 28. Kenny Lofton returned as a free agent after a one-year hiatus in Atlanta and had 64 RBI of his own.

But finding an ace continued to elude the Tribe. Charles Nagy and newly acquired Dave Burba won 15 games each. Bartolo Colon, tagged as the ace of the future, won 14, while Jaret Wright struggled to win 12. Closer Jose Mesa never recovered from his ninth-inning implosion in the 1997 World Series and was traded in July. In his place, Mike Jackson picked up 40 saves.

The ALDS pitted the Tribe against the Red Sox for the second time in four years. The results were the same. The Indians blew past Boston, taking the series three games to one. A playoff rematch with the Yankees awaited the Tribe.

The magic of Cleveland's 1997 ALDS win against New York failed to materialize again in 1998. A two-games-to-one advantage against the Yanks proved just an illusion as New York, winner of 114 regular-season

Jaret Wright, just a season removed from being a World Series hero, didn't survive the first inning of Game 1 of the 1998 ALCS against the Yankees. Taunted by Bronx cheers of "Jar-et, Jar-et," Wright was hammered for five runs in two-thirds of an inning.

David Justice sparkled in Cleveland, hitting 96 homers in three-plus seasons while helping fans forget Albert Belle. His trade to the New York Yankees in 2000 proved fruitful, too: The Indians received right-hander Jake Westbrook.

games, swept the next three games to dispatch the Tribe.

In the wake of the loss, a rivalry with the Yankees, dormant since the Indians heydays of the 1950s, was emerging again.

"This is a big rivalry for sure," Yankees manager Joe Torre said after his club's win.

The next year, 1999, brought more playoff anguish, despite the signing of star second baseman, Roberto Alomar. The Tribe bobbed and weaved through a plethora of injuries to win 97 games and their fifth straight division title. Once again, the Red Sox waited.

It looked like another easy road for Cleveland as the Indians took a 2–0 lead in the best-of-five series. Then panic set in. But it was Cleveland panicking, not the Red Sox.

The Indians found a way to blow the series, dropping three straight to the Sox while surrendering a record 23 runs in Game 4 and 12 more in the decisive Game 5. Tribe fans found solace in the fact that injuries caused their team to use 25 different pitchers during the season but couldn't stop them from winning another division title.

Akron *Beacon Journal* sportswriter Sheldon Ocker tried to soothe fans following the collapse against the Red Sox: "How could this happen?" he wrote. "The short answer is Cleveland finally ran out of mirrors."

Heavy Promise

Indians fans saw glimmers of greatness in Bartolo Colon. The Dominican fireplug used his thick legs to power 100-mph fastballs—his ticket out of the poverty in his homeland. That ticket got punched all the way to the front of the Indians' rotation.

Colon emerged as the team's ace in 1999, going 18–5. Still, Tribe fans wanted more. Colon responded with average seasons: 15 wins in 2000 and 14 in 2001. He fulfilled his promise in 2002, but he was somewhere else. Cleveland traded the pitcher to Montreal in midseason, a masterstroke that brought Grady Sizemore, Cliff Lee, and Brandon Phillips to Ohio. Colon won a combined 20 games in 2002 and signed with the Los Angeles Angels of Anaheim after the 2003 season. He won the 2005 Cy Young Award with the Halos.

Man, Oh, Manny

Indians teammates called Manny Ramirez "The Baby Bull" when he came to the majors in 1993 as a thin-legged, 21-year-old outfielder with a huge bat. Eight seasons later, "best hitter ever" became his moniker as he developed into one of the most feared batsmen ever to dig in at home plate.

Sure, he was quirky, a man-child with millions. Legend has it he asked a team attendant to wash his car. When the kid asked for a tip, Ramirez directed him to the glove compartment, where $10,000 in cash was inside.

Ramirez wasn't the fleetest afoot, nor was he the wisest baserunner. And defense was always an adventure. Then again, he was paid to hit, which he could definitely do—to all fields, for power and average.

Born in the Dominican Republic and raised in the roughest parts of New York City, Manny was a high school star and the Indians' first-round draft pick in 1991. He arrived in Cleveland two years later—with no money, no luggage, no equipment, and no worries. He forgot them all at the airport. Before long, he was the Indians' starting right fielder, batting low in a lineup filled with power.

"Wow," was all Oakland A's closer Dennis Eckersley could muster after Ramirez took the future Hall of Famer deep, smashing a game-winning homer in a 1995 game at Jacobs Field. That season Ramirez hit .308 with 31 home runs and 107 RBI. In 1999, he broke the Indians single-season RBI record, knocking in 165 runs, three better than Hal Trosky's total in 1936. Ramirez hit .333 that same season.

Ramirez's sometimes-lackadaisical attitude caused plenty of clubhouse tension. Cleveland said *adios* to the Manny sideshow before the 2001 season, when the slugger signed a free-agent deal with Boston. He wore out his welcome with the Red Sox and was traded to the Los Angeles Dodgers at the trading deadline in 2008.

ESPN chronicled Manny Ramirez's ride through the free-agent market in 2000 on its show *Outside the Lines*. The Indians offered a seven-year, $119 million contract, by far the highest in team history, but Boston's $200 million over 10 years proved too rich for new owner Larry Dolan.

When it came to playing the outfield or running the bases, Manny Ramirez was never confused with Willie Mays. But inside the batter's box, Ramirez was a stats monster. He hit .313 and clubbed 236 home runs as an Indian and is considered by many to be the best all-around hitter in team history.

120

This Second Baseman Second to None

Roberto Alomar brought all five of his tools to Cleveland. The second baseman hit for power and average and ran the bases with speed and intelligence. His glovework was flawless, and his rifle arm made close plays routine. Alomar's career résumé reads like a Hall of Fame plaque: 12 All-Star appearances, 10 Gold Gloves, and a .300 lifetime average.

"You watch him," New York Yankees shortstop Derek Jeter once said, "and he does everything right."

His home run for Baltimore in the 1996 ALDS, eight days after an ugly spitting incident with an umpire, ended the Indians' season. Alomar was suspended for the spitting episode, but an appeal put off the suspension until the start of the 1997 season, rather than for the playoffs, much to the angst of Tribe fans.

All was forgiven in 1999 when Alomar signed as a free agent with Cleveland, where he put up his best numbers while playing beside his brother, catcher Sandy Alomar, Jr. In three years as an Indian, Robbie hit .323, .310, and .336, while averaging 21 homers and 103 RBI. He also teamed with shortstop Omar Vizquel to form baseball's finest keystone combination.

Alomar's luster swiftly diminished after the Indians traded him to the New York Mets to trim payroll after the 2001 season. He bounced around until retiring before the 2005 season to await his call from Cooperstown.

Roberto Alomar was a terrific fielder on his own, but his pairing with Omar Vizquel made him part of what many call the greatest middle-infield duo of all time. Marveling at his Gold Glove infield, pitcher Charles Nagy said: "Have I seen a better pair? No. They work so well together, and they do some things that are amazing."

The Gold Standard for Infields

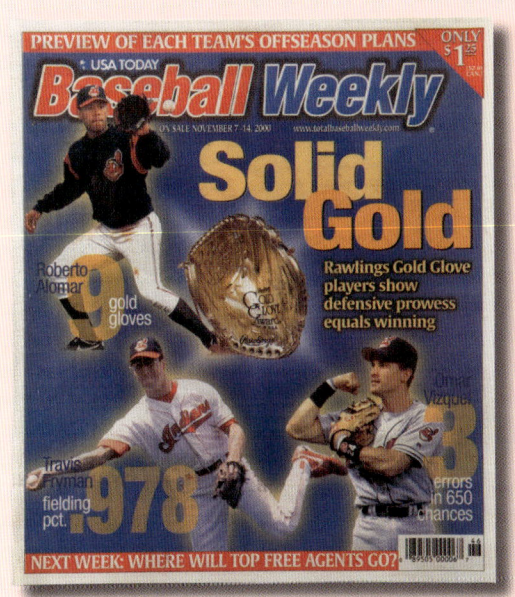

Ground balls didn't stand a chance against the 2000 Cleveland Indians infield—too much gold was in the way.

Third baseman Travis Fryman, shortstop Omar Vizquel, and second baseman Roberto Alomar all won Gold Gloves for their respective positions. Only the Baltimore Orioles infields of 1969 and 1971 matched the feat.

The 2000 trio committed just 26 errors during the season. For Fryman, the Gold Glove was his first in 11 seasons. Vizquel and Alomar were renowned glovemen. During their careers, Vizquel claimed 11 Gold Gloves while Alomar garnered 10.

The Beat Goes On

In the last row of the Municipal Stadium bleachers—section 55 to be exact—a small aluminum awning attached to the brick wall provided shelter for one special fan and his companion. John Adams has beaten his drum much longer than the roof the Indians provided in the 1970s held up. For 35 seasons, through lousy teams and World Series games, from the dregs of Municipal Stadium to the sparkles of Jacobs Field, Adams and his drum have played on.

The beating of his bass drum began harmlessly, with no intentions of reoccurrence, for an August 1973 game against the Texas Rangers. More than 2,600 games later, it's still heard.

"It's my Fantasy Island," Adams told a *New York Times* reporter. "It's my getaway from the real world."

Back when a bleacher seat cost a buck, Adams and his drum marched up the concrete steps to the top row. His goal was to drum up a little enthusiasm for a wretched team. He didn't intend to make it his life's work. Somehow, that's what it became.

Early on, few fans knew his name; instead, they called him "The Drummer." Over the years, Adams became a spokesman for Tribe fans. Out-of-town reporters looking for reflection on the team's attendance phenomenon in the 1990s needed only to speak to Adams as he sat at the top of the left-field bleachers at the Jake.

Adams estimates he has missed about three dozen games over the years. When heavy April snow in 2007 forced the Indians to play a home series in Milwaukee, the team paid for Adams and his drum to attend. That same year, when the Indians made the playoffs for the first time in six seasons, Adams was chosen to toss the ceremonial first pitch. The year before, Adams and his drum became a bobblehead promotion put on by the Indians. But instead of a head bobbing, the collectible statue's arms bounced onto a drum.

John Adams has beaten the same drum, which Herb Score nicknamed Big Chief Boom Boom, at Indians games for 35-plus years. He's rarely missed a contest and has paid his own way to almost every one, but not to an April 2007 game that was moved to Milwaukee because of snow in Cleveland (*pictured above*). Such devotion has earned the phone company computer technician a national reputation.

Superfan John Adams didn't have a bobblehead doll. His collectible—given away by the team as a promotion—was a bobblearm doll. "Being a drummer, I march to the beat of my own drum," he said.

122

Big Bucks and Big Expectations

Larry Dolan knew it coming in: Dick Jacobs would be some act to follow.

After buying the Indians in 1986, Jacobs had managed to achieve what previous Tribe owners had failed to do for 30 years: provide enough cash and business sense to make the Indians a winner in the standings and in the financial ledger. Unlike his predecessors, Jacobs understood that success in a small market would have to be built through a viable farm system. He also knew this meant spending money. His business model provided homegrown talent, but it was his business skills with local politicians that led to the team's renaissance as Cleveland built a new jewel of a ballpark.

By 1999, Jacobs was smart enough to know that his original $36 million purchase had maxed out. There were no more seats to be sold; every ticket was already bought. He knew his collection of All-Stars was aging and needed refueling.

There was no room for growth, only for rebuilding.

Dolan, a lifelong Clevelander and Indians fan, made his fortune as an attorney and by building a cable television empire with his brother, Charles. In 2000, he paid dearly for his home team: $323 million, plus the weight of replacing Jacobs.

In Dolan's first two seasons as owner, he spent more than the team ever had before. But revenues were sliding and the Indians were so riddled with injuries in 2000 that a record 23 different hurlers took the mound. Cleveland missed the playoffs in 2000 for the first time in five years. Dolan spent $96 million on the team's payroll in 2001, but they lost in the ALDS.

The natives were already growing restless, and the honeymoon with Dolan was ending. But the owner told reporters after a luncheon with impatient Indians fans that he understood the fans' passion. He also said he would be more worried if he didn't hear from them.

"When these people ask questions, they care," Dolan said. "They're not interested in my problems. They want to win."

Pundits say Richard Jacobs (*left*) showed his business savvy, selling the Indians at their financial peak, with little room for growth. Larry Dolan (*right*), a lifelong Indian fan, would soon endure a rebuilding.

CHAPTER SEVEN

Ready for Glory
2001—Today

AS A NEW century dawned, Indians fans comforted themselves with past successes, including five straight division titles and two World Series seasons. They knew that no other generation of Indians fans enjoyed so many triumphs, but they wanted more. They wanted the championship drought to end. And their Indians were changing. Dick Jacobs sold the club, Mike Hargrove was fired, and John Hart left for the Texas Rangers. Fans can only hope that the new architects finish the job.

Left: In the movie *Major League*, Indians first baseman Pedro Cerrano relied on Jobu for good luck. In real life, Tribe fans look for good fortune everywhere. *Above right:* Grady Sizemore's belt must be heavy because he carries all five tools. The Indians' leadoff man hits for power and average, runs like a deer, and brings a Gold Glove to his spot in center field. *Opposite:* Victor Martinez watches his home run sail into the seats of Fenway Park in Game 6 of the 2007 ALCS. Unfortunately for the Tribe, Boston won Games 5 through 7, by a combined score of 30–5, en route to the world title.

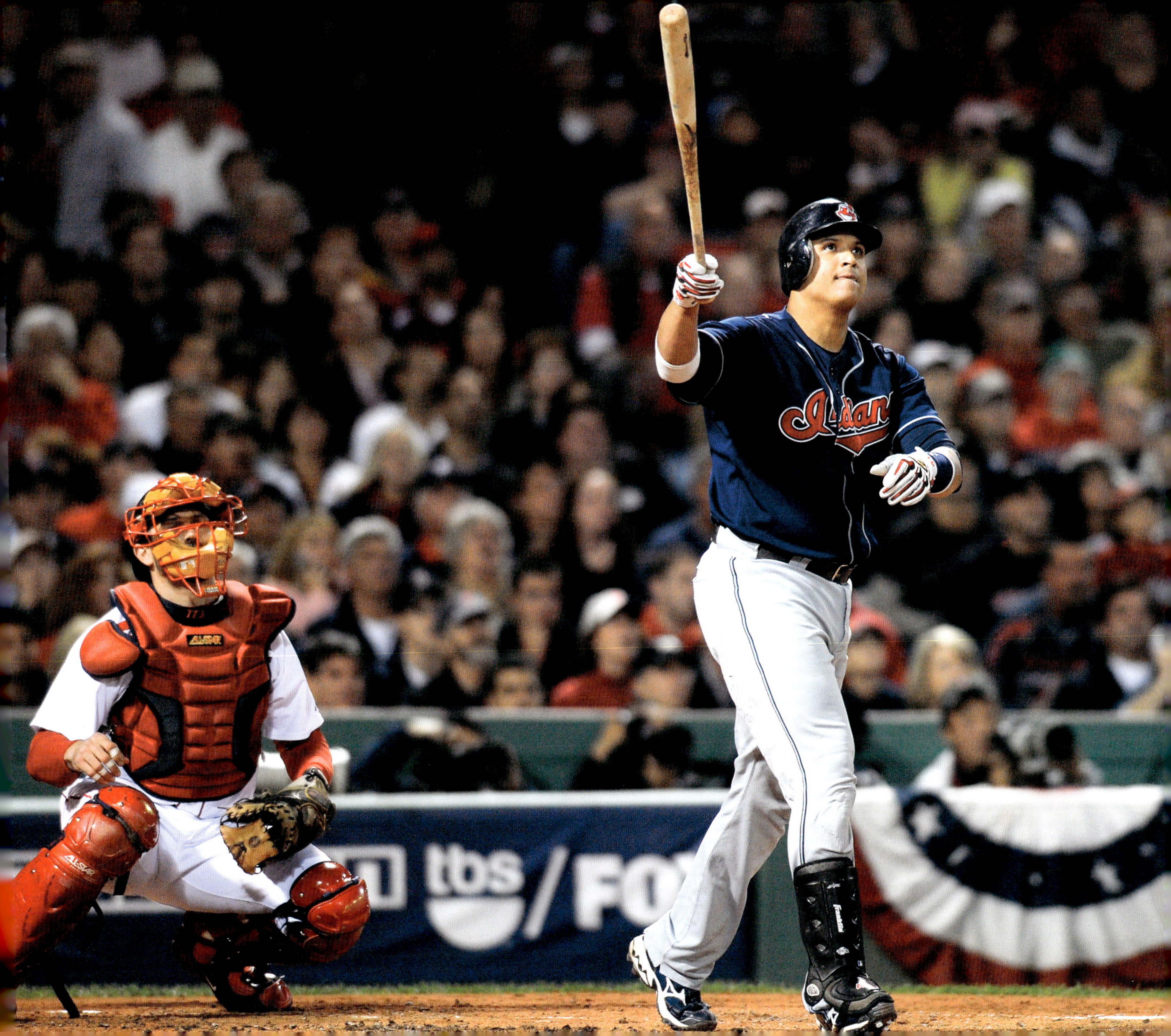
tbs

Last Gasp

The Indians delayed the inevitable rebuilding period for one more shot at the World Series. By 2001, the farm system that had cultivated so much talent was barren. Cleveland's star-studded lineup was aging. Manny Ramirez had bolted for Boston.

The Tribe compensated with free-agent outfielders Juan Gonzalez and Ellis Burks. On the mound, rookie left-hander CC Sabathia joined manager Charlie Manuel's rotation. The new faces paid dividends as Cleveland reclaimed the Central Division title, and attendance passed 3.1 million. The 116-win Seattle Mariners waited in the American League Division Series.

In Game 1, Bartolo Colon shut down the Mariners, and Burks homered as the Indians won 5–0. The Tribe couldn't solve Jamie Moyer in Game 2, and the Mariners won 5–1. After the Indians trounced Seattle 17–2 in Game 3, another trip to the ALCS seemed a lock. Colon was to pitch the next afternoon at the Jake for a chance to send the Mariners home.

Colon was tossing another shutout until the seventh inning when Seattle scored three runs on its way to a 6–2 win. Cleveland couldn't solve Moyer in Game 5, and the Mariners went on to take the series with a 3–1 win. With that loss, the Indians would embark on a new era: Reconstruction.

Epic Comeback

Radio dials were spinning. TV remotes were in full surf. Fans just taking their seats at Jacobs Field checked their watches. A 12–0 Seattle lead after three innings can do that.

The Indians couldn't just leave the field. Instead, they made history on August 5, 2001, when they recorded baseball's greatest comeback in 76 years. Trailing 14–2 after six, the Tribe scored three runs in the seventh and four in the eighth. Cleveland then scored five runs with two outs in the ninth to tie the game. Jolbert Cabrera's single in the 11th scored Kenny Lofton and delivered the 15–14 win.

"It's almost impossible to do, but they did it," marveled Mariners manager Lou Piniella.

Tribe catcher Einar Diaz scores in Game 3 of the 2001 ALDS against the Seattle Mariners at Jacobs Field. Every hitter in the Indians lineup scored as the Indians rolled 17–2.

The Thomenator

In his long big-league career, Jim Thome has traumatized many a pitcher's ERA with his powerful left-handed swing. Thome uses his bushy Popeye forearms to point his bat at the mound, as if to foreshadow the ensuing damage, but in truth, there is probably no nicer guy in the game.

Thome's 334 homers in his 12 years as an Indian put him atop the team's career leader board. He hit them high. He hit them often. He hit them when they counted, including 17 in the postseason. He also set the Indians' single-season record in 2002 with 52 round-trippers. Thome's 511-foot shot on July 3, 1999, still ranks as the longest in Jacobs Field history. It's no wonder fans called him "The Thomenator."

Thome was Cleveland's kind of guy, a 13th-round draft pick with an aw-shucks Midwestern drawl who clawed his way to the big leagues. He spoke to reporters while teammates ducked for cover. His batting helmet, which he tapped with his bat before every trip to the plate, was stained with pine tar—a symbol of his hard work. He even dressed as Santa Claus and delivered toys to underprivileged kids in the winter.

"He always tried to be the same old Jim who grew up in Peoria," wrote Amy Rosewater in her Thome biography, *Lefty Launcher*.

Thome came to Cleveland as a slim third baseman who reminded many of George Brett. He hit .314 with 25 homers in 1995, his first full season after four cups of coffee in the bigs. But Thome and his home run numbers grew as he moved to first base. He hit 49 homers in 2001, and his 52 homers the following season broke Albert Belle's single-season team mark.

But that would be the end of The Thomenator's reign in Cleveland. The slugger signed as a free agent with Philadelphia as the Tribe started rebuilding.

Jim Thome ranks among MLB's all-time leaders in home runs and RBI. While in Cleveland, the slugger brought his power to October, too, knocking out 17 dingers in 11 playoff series.

On a sometimes not-so-friendly team, Thome was the exception, to reporters and fans alike. In 2002, his humanitarian work earned him the Roberto Clemente Award.

JIM THOME HAD PLENTY TO SMILE ABOUT DURING HIS 12 SEASONS IN CLEVELAND. THOME'S BEST YEARS WERE SPENT NEXT TO LAKE ERIE, AND HE STILL HOLDS SEVERAL TEAM RECORDS.

THE 2002 INDIANS MAY NOT HAVE BEEN OUT OF THIS WORLD, BUT TO FANS, THE CLUB WAS HEROIC, AND THIS COMIC BOOK SERIES WAS PART OF THE PROMOTION.

THE INDIANS FOUND FAUSTO CARMONA, WHO AUTOGRAPHED THIS BALL, IN THE DOMINICAN REPUBLIC AND SIGNED HIM AS A FREE AGENT IN 2000. HE LANDED ON THE INDIANS' RADAR IN 2003 BY GOING 17-4 FOR THE LAKE COUNTY CAPTAINS IN SUBURBAN EASTLAKE.

THE INDIANS CELEBRATED THEIR 100TH ANNIVERSARY ALL SEASON LONG IN 2001. THE YEAR WAS HIGHLIGHTED BY THE SELECTION OF THE TEAM'S 100 GREATEST PLAYERS OF ALL TIME.

OFTEN-OVERLOOKED JHONNY PERALTA EMERGED FROM THE INDIANS' FARM SYSTEM TO REPLACE LEGENDARY SHORTSTOP OMAR VIZQUEL. IN 2005, HE HIT 24 HOMERS, THE MOST EVER BY AN INDIANS SHORTSTOP.

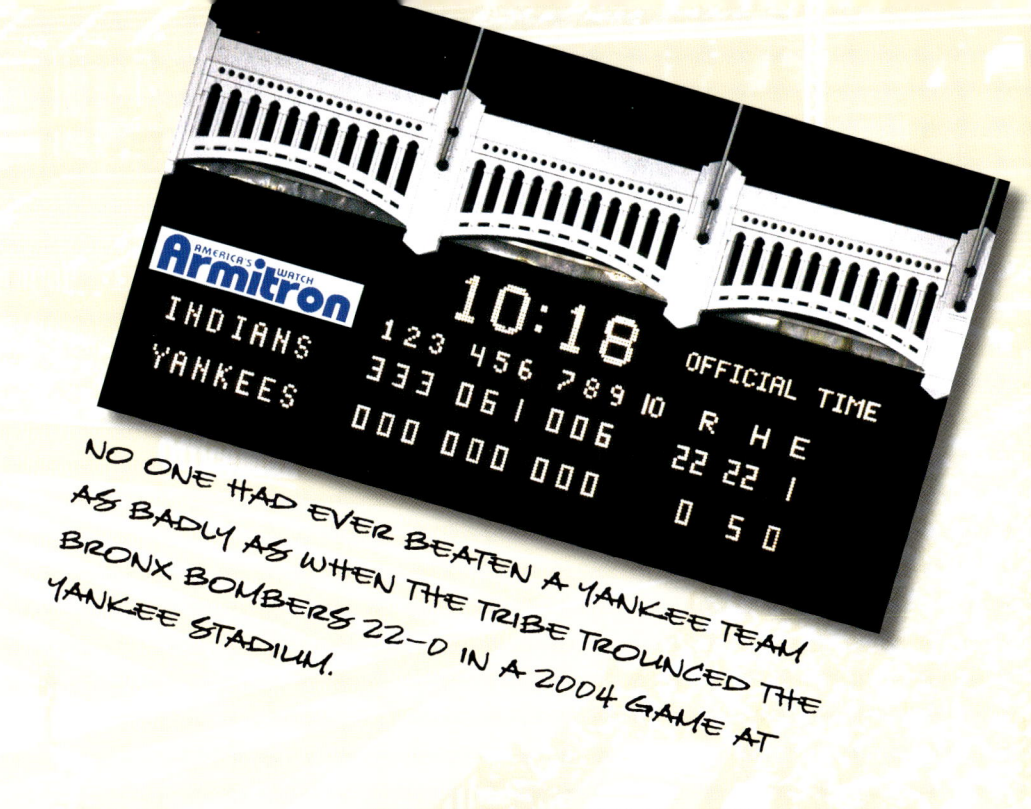

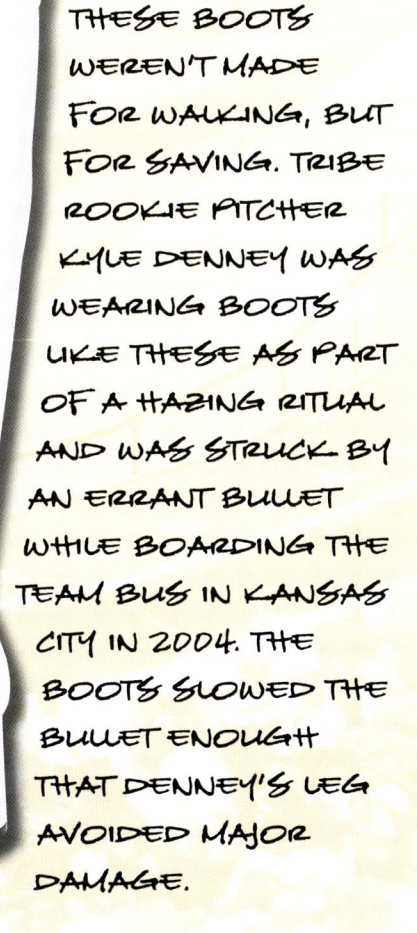

NO ONE HAD EVER BEATEN A YANKEE TEAM AS BADLY AS WHEN THE TRIBE TROUNCED THE BRONX BOMBERS 22-0 IN A 2004 GAME AT YANKEE STADIUM.

THESE BOOTS WEREN'T MADE FOR WALKING, BUT FOR SAVING. TRIBE ROOKIE PITCHER KYLE DENNEY WAS WEARING BOOTS LIKE THESE AS PART OF A HAZING RITUAL AND WAS STRUCK BY AN ERRANT BULLET WHILE BOARDING THE TEAM BUS IN KANSAS CITY IN 2004. THE BOOTS SLOWED THE BULLET ENOUGH THAT DENNEY'S LEG AVOIDED MAJOR DAMAGE.

THE WEATHER TO OPEN THE 2007 SEASON WAS FINE FOR SNOWMEN, BUT NOT FOR BASEBALL. THE EXTENDED WINTER FORCED THE INDIANS TO MOVE A HOME SERIES TO MILWAUKEE'S MILLER PARK, WHERE A RETRACTABLE ROOF OFFERED WARMTH.

The Man with the Plan

The Indians handed Mark Shapiro an aging club with a high payroll and few prospects when the new general manager took over for John Hart at the end of the 2001 season. Shapiro brought pedigree to the task as he rebuilt the Indians into contenders while twice winning the Executive of the Year Award from *The Sporting News*.

Shapiro grew up with baseball as the son of Baltimore-based sports agent Ron Shapiro. He took his first baseball job in Cleveland, landing there in 1991 shortly after graduating from Princeton. He ran the Tribe's farm system for five years and then served as Hart's assistant.

After 2001, there was talk that the Indians might rebuild on the fly instead of going through a complete overhaul. Shapiro's first move, he admitted, required a flack-jacket: a package trade that sent popular Roberto Alomar to the Mets for Matt Lawton, prospect Alex Escobar, and others. The retooling failed, and by midseason 2002, Operation Reconstruction went into full swing with the trade of Bartolo Colon to Montreal.

"Now I can start constructing a path toward another championship," Shapiro said.

In 2002, veteran left-hander Chuck Finley was traded to St. Louis for outfielder Coco Crisp. That off-season, catcher Einar Diaz and promising pitcher Ryan Drese were dealt to Texas for Travis Hafner. Shapiro signed utilityman Casey Blake and reliever Rafael Betancourt as free agents in 2003, and in 2002 and 2003, he drafted Ben Francisco, Ryan Garko, Kevin Kouzmanoff, and Aaron Laffey.

The Indians were contenders again by 2005—they won 93 games, only narrowly missing the playoffs despite having one of the lowest payrolls in baseball. Two seasons later, the Indians found themselves on the verge of another trip to the World Series.

"I think there is a reason why the Cleveland Indians have made a quick turnaround," Minnesota Twins GM Terry Ryan said. "[Shapiro's] got leadership qualities, and he thinks [about] things for the impact of the present, the near future, and the distant future."

In their first six seasons together, GM Mark Shapiro (*left*) and manager Eric Wedge saw the Tribe bounce around the Central Division, winning one title while finishing third or lower four times.

Left-handed Leviathan

Don't let the tilted cap, the cherub cheeks, and the girth fool you. Delivering a 95-mph fastball with pinpoint control from his rocket left arm, CC Sabathia is an imposing pitcher but also a terrific athlete.

American League hitters quickly learned this as Sabathia went 17–5 in 2001, his first season with the Tribe, and captured Rookie Pitcher of the Year honors from *The Sporting News*. Although he was just 20 years old, the 6'7", 290-pound Sabathia was about to become the anchor and ace of the Indians' pitching staff. By 2007, he was a three-time All-Star and a Cy Young Award winner. That season, he won 19, struck out 209, and walked just 37 while leading the Indians to their first ALCS in 10 years.

Sabathia, a three-sport high school standout from Vallejo, California, was Cleveland's first-round draft pick in 1998. Had he not been a pitcher, Sabathia may have been a prolific power hitter. During his eight-year stay in Cleveland, he won 106 games, but he also hit .300 with two home runs in 40 at-bats.

The Indians' disastrous start in 2008 and Sabathia's pending free agency prompted GM Mark Shapiro to trade the ace to Milwaukee for some top prospects. Disappointed fans hold out hope for a repeat of the bountiful Bartolo Colon trade of 2002.

Above: CC Sabathia could have played football in paradise, but he spurned a scholarship offer from the University of Hawaii to sign with the Indians as the 20th pick of the 1998 draft.

Ace in the Hole

He went 1–10 as a rookie in 2006, hardly drawing comparisons to Gene Bearden. But given another year, Fausto Carmona made believers out of doubting Tribe fans.

Carmona's neck ached his rookie season, not from injury, but from watching home runs fly as the Indians tried to make him a closer. He lost four games and blew three saves in *one week*. He surrendered nine homers in 38 appearances, but the following season an injury to Cliff Lee forced Carmona into the rotation. He delivered a 19–8 record, helping the Tribe reach the playoffs. The Indians rewarded the pitcher with a four-year contract.

Pronk Power

He runs like an injured wildebeest in a mudslide. Little Leaguers have better arms. The Terminal Tower has more range.

But few can hit like Travis Hafner.

Hafner broke through in 2004 with Thome-esque monster home runs. There were 28 in his first full season as an Indian, 33 the next season, and 42 in 2006 (tied with Jim Thome for third in the AL). His batting average topped .300 each year, and Hafner became a Cleveland favorite.

Hafner was never considered a top prospect, but GM Mark Shapiro saw enough to acquire the 6'3" North Dakotan from the Rangers in 2002 for the small price of pitcher Ryan Drese and catcher Einar Diaz. Teammates saw his promise, as well as his limits. In Hafner's first spring training with the Indians, reserve infielder Bill Selby labeled him "Pronk": part project and part donkey. Pronk, however, was all bat, as his weak arm and limited infield range made him the perfect designated hitter.

In mid-2007, Shapiro signed Hafner to a four-year, $57 million contract extension. By season's end, Hafner, despite hitting just 24 homers, still managed 100 RBI, the fourth straight year he met that power-hitting milestone. A shoulder injury hampered Hafner's production in 2008, but fans hope his recovery can help spur an Indian rebound.

"Anybody who watches this team play understands its resiliency, toughness, and work ethic," Shapiro said. "Haf personifies those things."

Travis Hafner had a grand time before the 2006 All-Star break, smacking a record five grand slams prior to the midsummer classic. Despite his stats, Pronk has never made an All-Star Team.

Best of the Backstops

The search for a catcher who hits for power and average starts and ends with Victor Martinez. The Venezuela native became the jewel of the Indians' resurgence in 2004 when he made the AL's Silver Slugger team, hitting .283 with 23 homers and 108 RBI in his first full season in Cleveland. Three .300 seasons followed for the switch-hitter, including a tremendous 2007: a .301 average, 25 homers, and 114 RBI. Mark Shapiro saw the promise and locked Martinez into a five-year contract in 2005.

"There's a premium for the position he plays and the teammate he is, and I think the leader he is going to become on this team," Shapiro marveled.

Face of the Franchise

After 256 at-bats in Class-A ball, he was hitting .258 with no home runs, hardly the kind of stats that project a future All-Star. The 19-year-old's numbers didn't overwhelm Indians GM Mark Shapiro, either. He never targeted Grady Sizemore when he dealt Bartolo Colon to the Montreal Expos in 2002. But Shapiro took the kid, almost as a throw-in compared to Cliff Lee and Brandon Phillips, the prized prospects harvested from the Colon trade.

For once, fate kissed the Indians.

The deal has become Shapiro's signature trade, as Sizemore's combination of speed, power, and defense make Shapiro look like the second coming of Branch Rickey.

"Everything about [Sizemore] sticks out," Tribe manager Eric Wedge said in 2006. "His athleticism, his energy level, his discipline. Everything. What Grady has is rare in this game."

An injury to Juan Gonzalez opened the door for Sizemore in 2005. The kid seized the opportunity by socking 22 home runs, hitting 37 doubles, legging out 11 triples, and swiping 22 bases, joining Roberto Alomar as the Indians' only 20–20–20–10 players. In 2006, his 134 runs scored, 92 extra-base hits, and 53 doubles topped the AL. Plus, the young ironman played every game. He made consecutive All-Star appearances from 2006 to 2008, won Gold Gloves in 2007 and 2008, and led the Indians to victory in the 2007 ALDS with his .375 batting average against the Yankees. In 2008, he joined Joe Carter as the only Indians ever to hit 30 homers and steal 30 bases in the same season.

Sizemore's popularity knows no limits, especially with women. In fact, a throng of female fans call themselves "Grady's Ladies." Marriage proposals come through the mail.

"It still shocks me," Sizemore said. "Some of these women are crazy."

But Shapiro obviously wasn't when he accepted this future franchise player as part of the Colon deal.

Grady's Ladies isn't just a T-shirt logo. A website of the same name gives fans a chance to learn and see more of the Indians' most eligible bachelor.

Some guys have all the luck: Grady Sizemore, Cleveland's young, handsome, and talented center fielder, was named the city's favorite Indian and its sexiest male celebrity in a 2008 poll by Cleveland Magazine.

Too Close for Comfort

As the 2007 season started, Tribe fans could neither spell nor pronounce Asdrubal and Fausto. And they couldn't envision another World Series, not after the poor showing in 2006.

Baseball is funny that way.

Mark Shapiro only tinkered with the 2007 team, adding second baseman Josh Barfield and reliever Joe Borowski. Prized rookie Ryan Garko won the first base job, and the team remained jammed with hard-hitting youngsters, like Jhonny Peralta, Grady Sizemore, Travis Hafner, and Victor Martinez. CC Sabathia, Cliff Lee, and Jake Westbrook headed the rotation.

A 17–8 start put the Indians atop the Central Division. The early going also saw the emergence of Fausto Carmona, who established himself as the team's No. 2 starter, just one season after his historic bullpen implosion in which he suffered five losses in nine games in his failed bid to replace traded closer Bob Wickman. After falling as low as fourth place, the Indians reclaimed the lead in August as slick-fielding Asdrubal Cabrera took over for Barfield at second base.

A forlorn Tribe bench is a sight that has been seen too often. Fans had visions of a World Series dashed from their dreams as the 2007 Boston Red Sox became just the 10th team ever to come back from a three-games-to-one playoff deficit.

The Tribe never looked back, and Clevelanders enjoyed October baseball for the first time in six seasons. In Cleveland, the postseason usually means two things: the Yankees and the Red Sox.

New York came first in the ALDS as the Tribe handed the Yanks a pair of defeats at the Jake. In Game 1, Garko, Cabrera, Martinez, and Hafner homered to offset Sabathia's wildness in a 12–3 win. Carmona sparkled in Game 2 amid a swarm of midges. He surrendered only one run on three hits as the Indians won 2–1 in 11 innings on a Hafner single. The Yankees won Game 3 in the Bronx, but the Tribe ended the series the next night with a 6–4 win.

Only the Red Sox stood in the way of an improbable World Series.

Boston bombed Sabathia and the Indians 10–3 in Game 1 at Fenway Park. Game 2 began ominously as Carmona was rocked, but the Cleveland hitters saved the Indians, pulling out a 13–6 victory.

Wins by Paul Byrd and Westbrook put the Indians ahead in the best-of-seven series 3–1. World Series fever was once again palpable. And why not? Sabathia and Carmona, two 19-game winners, stood in the wings with the Tribe needing just one more win. It wouldn't come—Boston would outscore the Tribe 30–5 in the next three games.

Sabathia's postseason blues continued in Game 5 as he was pounded in a 7–1 Red Sox win. Carmona fared worse, surrendering seven runs in two innings of a 12–2 pasting in Game 6. Westbrook couldn't stop the bleeding as the Tribe's collapse came full circle with an 11–2 shellacking.

"We needed something special to happen," third baseman Casey Blake said. "We needed things to go our way, and they didn't."

Bugged Out

Cleveland had several large and intimidating players in their 2007 lineup, but the Yankees' biggest nemeses in Game 2 of the 2007 American League Division Series were tiny bugs. With the Tribe trailing 1–0 in the eighth and fireballing Yankee rookie Joba Chamberlain on the Jake's mound, a swarm of Lake Erie midges descended.

The little pests would alter the game and the series.

"It was miserable," Chamberlain recalled. "They were everywhere."

The bugs dotted Chamberlain's neck, walked on his forehead, and climbed into his ears. Insect repellent was useless, and Chamberlain came unglued. He walked two, hit a batter, and uncorked two wild pitches, the last of which scored Grady Sizemore to tie the game. Indians pitcher Fausto Carmona wasn't rattled. He kept the Yankees in check, allowing the Tribe to win in the 11th.

Far left: Steady Jake Westbrook pitched the Indians to a win in Game 3 of the ALCS and bulldogged his way through six innings of Game 7. But the Tribe's bullpen imploded in the final two innings, giving up eight runs as the Red Sox ran off to the World Series with an 11-2 win. *Left:* It was shocking. Needing just one win, Cleveland hitters managed a paltry five runs in the final three games of the ALCS while Boston cranked out 30.

WHO SAYS YOU CAN'T TAKE GRADY SIZEMORE HOME WITH YOU? THE INDIANS CAPITALIZED ON THEIR STAR OUTFIELDER'S POPULARITY, CREATING AN ASSORTMENT OF MEMORABILIA, INCLUDING A VARIETY OF BOBBLEHEADS.

CLIFF LEE AVERAGED MORE THAN 15 WINS A SEASON FROM 2004 TO 2006 BEFORE HE HURT HIS ARM IN 2007. HIS COMEBACK SEASON IN 2008 GAVE HIM THE MOST WINS (22) BY AN INDIAN LEFT-HANDER SINCE VEAN GREGG IN 1911.

DESPITE HIS IMPRESSIVE SIZE, CC SABATHIA IS AN ATHLETE WITH MOVES. IN 2007, THE INDIANS PROMOTED THE BYGONE DISCO ERA, OFFERING A GROOVY RENDITION OF A SABATHIA BOBBLEHEAD DOLL.

PLAYING OFF THE INCREDIBLE HULK THEME, YOUNG INDIANS FANS RECEIVED A GREEN-COLOR WOODEN BAT BEARING TRAVIS HAFNER'S SIGNATURE DURING A PROMOTION AT JACOBS FIELD IN 2007.

136

The Indians keep on rolling and searching through a truckload of dreams for the World Series championship that has eluded them for more than 60 summers.

The Indians sold the ballpark's naming rights to Progressive Insurance before the 2008 season, and fans are still debating what to call the newly named yard. "The Prog" just doesn't have the same ring as "The Jake."

#48 TRAVIS HAFNER

137

Still Waiting

Indians fans know their team's history is riddled with woulda, coulda, shoulda seasons. The Tribe's much-anticipated 2008 campaign didn't deviate from the story. The team that finished so close to the World Series the year before weathered ups and downs to finish at a mediocre-defining 81–81.

Would they have fared better without injuries to Travis Hafner, Victor Martinez, Fausto Carmona, and Jake Westbrook? Could the Indians have picked up a free-agent slugger in the off-season? Should the team have waited to trade CC Sabathia, Casey Blake, and Paul Byrd?

After flirting with last place for much of the summer, the Tribe won 44 of the final 74 games to finish in third place, 7½ games back of the Chicago White Sox. The surge left fans wondering, but not manager Eric Wedge.

"I never look at what could have been," Wedge told reporters.

As it was, Cleveland fans placated themselves as they marveled at the historic season enjoyed by pitcher Cliff Lee, the AL's Cy Young Award winner and Comeback Player of the Year. The southpaw fashioned an AL-best 22–3 record to go with his 2.54 earned run average. He even started the All-Star Game.

After a slow start in 2008, first baseman Ryan Garko went on an RBI bender, knocking in 45 runs and hitting .319 in his final 57 games. He finished the year with 90 RBI, tying Grady Sizemore for the team lead.

Cliff Lee didn't even make the Indians' postseason roster in 2007, but in 2008 he had one of the best pitching seasons in team history. Lee went 22–3, becoming the Indians' first 20-game winner since Gaylord Perry in 1974.

With injuries to Travis Hafner and Victor Martinez, shortstop Jhonny Peralta moved into the cleanup spot late in the 2008 season. His 23 homers and 89 RBI placed him among baseball's best-hitting shortstops.

Grady Sizemore continued to show he's one of baseball's most dynamic five-tool talents. With 33 home runs and 38 steals, Sizemore joined Joe Carter as the only members of the Indians' 30–30 club. The center fielder scored 101 runs and knocked in 90 himself from the top of the Tribe lineup.

Shortstop Jhonny Peralta's 23 homers and 89 RBI led all AL shortstops, and his keystone mate, Asdrubal Cabrera, pulled off the Tribe's first unassisted triple play since Bill Wambsganss in the 1920 World Series. An early-season batting slump put Cabrera back in the minors, but the second baseman reclaimed his spot in July and hit .320 the rest of the way. First baseman Ryan Garko rediscovered his power stroke and tied Sizemore for the team lead in RBI.

Kelly Shoppach filled in for Martinez to lead AL catchers with 21 home runs. And outfielder Shin-Soo Choo showed promise in the second half, finishing the year with a team-high .309 average, 14 dingers, and 66 RBI.

But it was poor pitching that thwarted the Tribe's chances right out of the gate. Aside from Lee, no Indian starter won more than eight games. Carmona, coming off a 19-win season, and the always-reliable Westbrook, each went down with injuries. Set-up man Rafael Betancourt, almost untouched a year before, struggled all year. Closer Joe Borowski didn't come close to duplicating his 2007 success and was released on July 4.

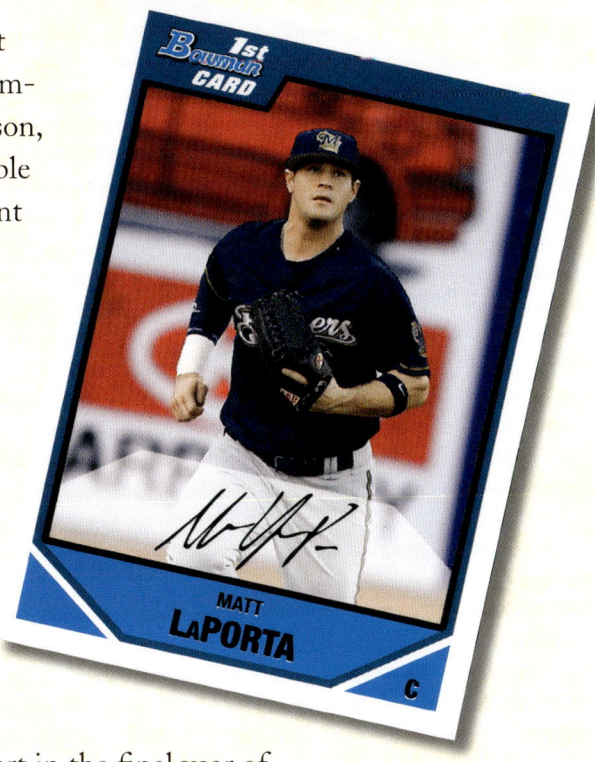

Sabathia's slow start in the final year of his contract mirrored the team's poor showing. The big man's trade to Milwaukee on July 7 for heralded prospects Matt LaPorta and Michael Brantley was the white flag. Byrd and Blake, who were also looking at free agency, were traded, too.

"You take away any team's No. 2 and No. 3 starter and No. 3 and No. 4 hitters and they're screwed," Lee said.

Losing so many top-flight players to early-season slumps and injuries sunk the Tribe's chances in '08. However, the team's second-half surge left fans, as usual, hopeful for next year.

"I want to utilize what we learned this year [and] take it out for a spin in 2009," Wedge said.

Cleveland fans will certainly provide the championship drive.

The prize of the CC Sabathia trade, blue-chip prospect Matt LaPorta, hit 34 home runs with 105 RBI in just 131 minor-league games in 2007 and 2008.

CHAPTER 8

LEADERS AND LEGENDS

Team History

Nicknames
Blues (1901)
Bronchos (1902)
Naps (1903–1914)
Indians (1915–Present)

World Series Winners
1920, 1948

Pennant Winners
1920, 1948, 1954, 1995, 1997

American League Central Division Winners
1995, 1996, 1997, 1998, 1999, 2001, 2007

Ballparks
League Park/Dunn Field (1891–1947)
Cleveland Municipal Stadium (1932–1993)
Jacobs Field/Progressive Field (1994–Present)

Hall of Famers

(by primary position; years with Indians indicated)

Earl Averill, CF, 1929–1939
Lou Boudreau, SS, 1938–1950
Steve Carlton, P, 1987
Stan Coveleski, P, 1916–1924
Larry Doby, CF, 1947–1955, 1958
Dennis Eckersley, P, 1975–1977
Bob Feller, P, 1936–1941, 1945–1956
Elmer Flick, CF, 1902–1910
Addie Joss, P, 1902–1910
Ralph Kiner, LF, 1955
Nap Lajoie, 2B, 1902–1914
Bob Lemon, P, 1941–1942, 1946–1958
Eddie Murray, 1B, 1994–1996
Hal Newhouser, P, 1954–1955
Phil Niekro, P, 1986–1987
Satchel Paige, P, 1948–1949
Gaylord Perry, P, 1972–1975
Sam Rice, RF, 1934
Frank Robinson, RF, 1974–1977
Joe Sewell, SS, 1920–1930
Tris Speaker, CF, 1916–1926
Hoyt Wilhelm, P, 1957–1958
Dave Winfield, RF, 1995
Early Wynn, P, 1949–1957, 1963
Cy Young, P, 1909–1911

Non-players
Walter Johnson, manager, 1933–1935 (inducted as a pitcher)
Al Lopez, manager, 1951–1956
Bill Veeck, Jr., owner/executive, 1946–1949

Retired Uniform Numbers

3-Earl Averill
5-Lou Boudreau
14-Larry Doby
18-Mel Harder
19-Bob Feller
21-Bob Lemon
42-Jackie Robinson*
455-The Fans**

*Retired by all major-league clubs
**In honor of record 455 consecutive sellouts at Jacobs Field

The first game the Indians played in Jacobs Field was actually an exhibition contest against the Pittsburgh Pirates on April 2, 1994.

Award Winners

AL MVP
George Burns, 1B, 1926
Lou Boudreau, SS, 1948
Al Rosen, 3B, 1953

AL Cy Young Award
Gaylord Perry, 1972
CC Sabathia, 2007
Cliff Lee, 2008

AL Rookie of the Year
Herb Score, P, 1955
Chris Chambliss, 1B, 1971
Joe Charboneau, LF/DH, 1980
Sandy Alomar, Jr., C, 1990

Gold Glove
Vic Power, 1B, 1958, 1959, 1960, 1961
Minnie Minoso, OF, 1959
Jimmy Piersall, OF, 1961
Vic Davalillo, OF, 1964
Ray Fosse, C, 1970, 1971
Rick Manning, OF, 1976
Sandy Alomar, Jr., C, 1990
Kenny Lofton, OF, 1993, 1995, 1996
Omar Vizquel, SS, 1994, 1995, 1996, 1997, 1998, 1999, 2000, 2001

140

Matt Williams, 3B, 1997
Roberto Alomar, 2B, 1999, 2000, 2001
Travis Fryman, 3B, 2000
Grady Sizemore, OF, 2007, 2008

Silver Slugger
Andre Thornton, DH, 1984
Julio Franco, 2B, 1988
Carlos Baerga, 2B, 1993, 1994
Albert Belle, OF, 1993, 1994, 1995, 1996
Manny Ramirez, OF, 1995, 1999, 2000
Jim Thome, 3B, 1996
David Justice, OF, 1997
Matt Williams, 3B, 1997
Roberto Alomar, 2B, 1999, 2000
Juan Gonzalez, OF, 2001
Victor Martinez, OF, 2004
Grady Sizemore, OF, 2008

AL Manager of the Year
Eric Wedge, 2007

Batting Records

American League Leaders (= tied)*

Batting Average
Nap Lajoie, 1902 - .378 (part of season spent with Philadelphia A's)
Nap Lajoie, 1903 - .344
Nap Lajoie, 1904 - .376
Elmer Flick, 1905 - .308
Nap Lajoie, 1910 - .384
Tris Speaker, 1916 - .386
Lew Fonseca, 1929 - .369
Lou Boudreau, 1944 - .327
Bobby Avila, 1954 - .341

Home Runs
Braggo Roth, 1915 - 7 (part of season spent with Chicago White Sox)
Al Rosen, 1950 - 37
Larry Doby, 1952 - 32
Al Rosen, 1953 - 43
Larry Doby, 1954 - 32
Rocky Colavito, 1959 - 42 *
Albert Belle, 1995 - 50

Runs Batted In
Nap Lajoie, 1904 - 102
Hal Trosky, 1936 - 162
Al Rosen, 1952 - 105
Al Rosen, 1953 - 145
Larry Doby, 1954 - 126
Rocky Colavito, 1965 - 108
Joe Carter, 1986 - 121
Albert Belle, 1993 - 129
Albert Belle, 1995 - 126 *
Albert Belle, 1996 - 148
Manny Ramirez, 1999 - 165

Career Team Batting Leaders (Top Five)

Average
Joe Jackson - .375
Tris Speaker - .354
Nap Lajoie - .339
George Burns - .327
Ed Morgan - .323

Runs Scored
Earl Averill - 1,154
Tris Speaker - 1,079
Kenny Lofton - 975
Charlie Jamieson - 942
Jim Thome - 917

Hits
Nap Lajoie - 2,046
Tris Speaker - 1,965
Earl Averill - 1,903
Joe Sewell - 1,800
Charlie Jamieson - 1,753

Doubles
Tris Speaker - 486
Nap Lajoie - 424
Earl Averill - 377
Joe Sewell - 375
Lou Boudreau - 367

Early in his career, Albert Belle was known as Joey, his childhood nickname. He started using Albert after undergoing counseling for alcohol abuse.

Triples
Earl Averill - 121
Tris Speaker - 108
Elmer Flick - 106
Joe Jackson - 89
Jeff Heath - 83

Home Runs
Jim Thome - 334
Albert Belle - 242
Manny Ramirez - 236
Earl Averill - 226
Hal Trosky - 216

Runs Batted In
Earl Averill - 1,084
Jim Thome - 927
Nap Lajoie - 919
Hal Trosky - 911
Tris Speaker - 884

Stolen Bases
Kenny Lofton - 452
Omar Vizquel - 279
Terry Turner - 254
Nap Lajoie - 240
Ray Chapman - 233

Pitching Records

American League Leaders (= tied)*

Victories
Addie Joss, 1907 - 27 *
Jim Bagby, 1920 - 31

George Uhle, 1923 - 26
George Uhle, 1926 - 27
Bob Feller, 1939 - 24
Bob Feller, 1940 - 27
Bob Feller, 1941 - 25
Bob Feller, 1946 - 26 *
Bob Feller, 1947 - 20
Bob Lemon, 1950 - 23
Bob Feller, 1951 - 22
Early Wynn, 1954 - 23 *
Bob Lemon, 1954 - 23 *
Bob Lemon, 1955 - 18 *
Jim Perry, 1960 - 18 *
Gaylord Perry, 1972 - 24 *
Cliff Lee, 2008 - 22

Earned Run Average
Earl Moore, 1903 - 1.74
Addie Joss, 1904 - 1.59
Addie Joss, 1908 - 1.16
Vean Gregg, 1911 - 1.80
Stan Coveleski, 1923 - 2.76
Mel Harder, 1933 - 2.95
Bob Feller, 1940 - 2.61
Gene Bearden, 1948 - 2.43
Mike Garcia, 1949 - 2.36
Early Wynn, 1950 - 3.20
Mike Garcia, 1954 - 2.64
Sam McDowell, 1965 - 2.18
Luis Tiant, 1968 - 1.60
Rick Sutcliffe, 1982 - 2.96
Kevin Millwood, 2005 - 2.86
Cliff Lee, 2008 - 2.54

Strikeouts
Stan Coveleski, 1920 - 133
Bob Feller, 1938 - 240
Bob Feller, 1939 - 246
Bob Feller, 1940 - 261
Bob Feller, 1941 - 260
Allie Reynolds, 1943 - 151
Bob Feller, 1946 - 348
Bob Feller, 1947 - 196
Bob Feller, 1948 - 164
Bob Lemon, 1950 - 170
Herb Score, 1955 - 245
Herb Score, 1956 - 263
Early Wynn, 1957 - 184
Sam McDowell, 1965 - 325
Sam McDowell, 1966 - 225
Sam McDowell, 1968 - 283
Sam McDowell, 1969 - 279
Sam McDowell, 1970 - 304
Len Barker, 1980 - 187
Len Barker, 1981 - 127

Career Team Pitching Leaders (Top Five)

Victories
Bob Feller - 266
Mel Harder - 223
Bob Lemon - 207
Stan Coveleski - 172
Early Wynn - 164

Earned Run Average
Addie Joss - 1.89
Glenn Liebhardt - 2.17
Vean Gregg - 2.31
Bob Rhoads - 2.39
Bill Bernhard - 2.45

Strikeouts
Bob Feller - 2,581
Sam McDowell - 2,159
Bob Lemon - 1,277
Early Wynn - 1,277
CC Sabathia - 1,265

Shutouts
Addie Joss - 45
Bob Feller - 44
Stan Coveleski - 31
Bob Lemon - 31
Mike Garcia - 27
Mel Harder - 25

Saves
Bob Wickman - 139
Doug Jones - 129
Jose Mesa - 104
Mike Jackson - 94
Ray Narleski - 53

No-Hit Games
Bob Rhoads vs. Boston, September 18, 1908, 2–0
Addie Joss vs. Chicago, October 2, 1908, 1–0 (Perfect Game)
Addie Joss at Chicago, April 20, 1910, 1–0
Ray Caldwell at New York, September 10, 1919, 3–0
Wes Ferrell vs. St. Louis, April 29, 1931, 9–0
Bob Feller at Chicago, April 16, 1940, 1–0
Don Black vs. Philadelphia, July 10, 1947, 3–0
Bob Feller vs. New York, April 30, 1946, 1–0
Bob Lemon at Detroit, June 30, 1948, 2–0
Bob Feller vs. Detroit, July 1, 1951, 2–1
Sonny Siebert vs. Washington, June 10, 1966, 2–0
Dick Bosman at Oakland, July 19, 1974, 4–0
Dennis Eckersley vs. California, May 30, 1977, 1–0
Len Barker vs. Toronto, May 15, 1981, 3–0 (Perfect Game)

Indians All-Time Lineup

Catcher
Steve O'Neill 1911–1923

First base
Jim Thome 1991–2002

Second base
Nap Lajoie 1902–1914

Third base
Al Rosen 1947–1956

Shortstop
Omar Vizquel 1994–2004

Outfielders
Earl Averill 1929–1939
Tris Speaker 1916–1926
Manny Ramirez 1993–2000

Pitcher
Bob Feller 1936–1941, 1945–56

Index

A
Aaron, Hank, 103
Adams, John, 122
Agee, Tommie, 71
Alexander, Grover Cleveland, 54
Allen, Johnny, 33
Alomar, Roberto, 111, 116, 119, 121, 130, 133
Alomar, Sandy, Jr., 9, 95, 112, 116, 121
Alomar, Sandy, Sr., 116
Alvis, Max, 75, 76
Anderson, Brian, 111
Antonelli, Johnny, 61
Armour, Bill, 14
Aspromonte, Ken, 87, 88
Averill, Earl, 32–33, 35, 37
Avery, Steve, 107
Avila, Bobby, 38, 60–61, 64–65, 76

B
Baerga, Carlos, 95, 99, 111
Bagby, Jim, Jr., 43
Bagby, Jim, Sr., 25, 26–27, 30
Ballparks
    Camden Yards, 103, 111
    Case Commons, 12
    Cleveland Municipal Stadium, 8, 22, 34–35, 36–37, 42, 47, 49, 52–53, 55, 56, 61, 68, 69, 72, 73, 74–75, 76, 78–79, 84–85, 87, 92, 93, 95, 96–97, 98, 99, 102, 106, 108, 113, 122
    Comiskey Park, 49, 104
    Ebbets Field, 26
    Fenway Park, 81, 124–25, 135
    Jacobs Field (Progressive Field), 6, 9, 35, 100–01, 102, 106–07, 108–09, 110, 111, 112–13, 114, 116–17, 120, 122, 126, 127, 135, 136–37
    Kennard Street Park, 13
    Kingdome, 107
    League Park (Dunn Field), 10, 13, 14, 15, 18, 19, 20, 22, 25, 27, 29, 31, 32, 36–37, 40, 49, 102
    Memorial Stadium, 71
    Miller Park, 129
    New Orleans Superdome, 82
    Polo Grounds, 24, 28, 61
    Riverfront Stadium, 81
    Tiger Stadium, 69
    Yankee Stadium, 91, 129
Barfield, Josh, 134
Barker, Len, 8–9, 92, 93, 96
Barnard, Ernest, 36
Barnum, P. T., 46
Bearden, Gene, 51, 52–53, 131
Beene, Fred, 83
Bell, Buddy, 8–9, 83
Bell, "Cool Papa," 49
Bell, Gary, 65
Belle, Albert, 99, 100, 104, 108, 111, 112, 119, 127
Bellhorn, Mark, 99
Bench, Johnny, 81
Berardino, Johnny, 55
Betancourt, Rafael, 130, 139
Bishop, Max, 37
Black, Don, 44
Blake, Casey, 130, 135, 138–39
Bond, Walter, 68
Bonda, Ted, 89
Bonds, Bobby, 92
Borowski, Joe, 134, 139
Bosman, Dick, 84
Boudreau, Lou, 38–39, 45, 47, 49, 50, 51, 52–53, 56, 57, 70, 110, 114
Boyd, Dennis "Oil Can," 92
Bradley, Alva, 32, 36–37, 40, 42, 50, 94
Bragan, Bobby, 62, 70
Brantley, Michael, 139
Brett, George, 93, 127
Brown, Jackie, 90
Brown, Larry, 73
Buhner, Jay, 107, 114
Burba, Dave, 115, 118
Burkett, Jesse, 13
Burks, Ellis, 126
Burns, George, 30, 31
Burroughs, Jeff, 87
Bush, George, 93
Buskey, Tom, 83
Byrd, Paul, 135, 138–39

C
Cabrera, Asdrubal, 134–35, 139
Cabrera, Jolbert, 126
Caldwell, Ray, 26, 30
Camden Yards. See Ballparks.
Camper, Cardell, 91
Carew, Rod, 93
Carey, Drew, 106
Carlton, Steve, 96
Carmona, Fausto, 128, 131, 134–35, 138–39
Carrasquel, Chico, 65
Carter, Gary, 93
Carter, Joe, 95, 97, 133, 139
Carty, Rico, 89
Case Commons. See Ballparks.
Casey, Sean, 115
Cash, Norm, 70
Chamberlain, Joba, 135
Chambliss, Chris, 82, 83
Chance, Bob, 74
Chapman, Ray, 22, 24, 25, 26–27, 28–29
Charboneau, "Super Joe," 91, 96
Choo, Shin-Soo, 139
Chylak, Nestor, 87
Clemens, Roger, 107
Cleveland Municipal Stadium. See Ballparks.
Clinton, Bill, 103
Cobb, Ty, 14, 15, 16, 19
Cochrane, Mickey, 37
Colavito, Rocky, 62, 65, 67, 68, 69, 70, 71, 80, 95
Collins, Eddie, 19
Colon, Bartolo, 112, 118–19, 126, 130, 131, 133
Comiskey Park. See Ballparks.
Corrales, Pat, 94
Counsell, Craig, 113
Coveleski, Stan, 25, 26–27, 30
Cox, Ted, 83
Crews, Laurie, 98
Crews, Tim, 98
Crisp, Coco, 130

D
Darvas, Lou, 67, 73, 80
Dean, Dizzy, 6
DeLeon, Jose, 97
Demeter, Steve, 70
Denney, Kyle, 129
Diaz, Bo, 83, 93
Diaz, Einar, 126, 130, 132
DiMaggio, Joe, 40, 42
Doby, Larry, 7, 38, 43, 47, 48–49, 52–53, 60–61, 64, 78, 110
Dolan, Larry, 120, 123
Dolgan, Bob, 59
Drese, Ryan, 130, 132
Dudley, Jimmy, 59
Duffy, Frank, 86
Dunn, Edith, 31
Dunn, "Sunny Jim," 20–21, 29, 31, 36
Dunn Field. See League Park. See also Ballparks.
Durocher, Leo, 57
Dyer, Bob, 113
Dykes, Jimmy, 70

E
Earley, Joe, 47
Easter, Luke, 38, 56
Ebbets Field. See Ballparks.
Eckersley, Dennis, 8, 83, 89, 106, 120
Eckhouse, Morris, 61
Edwards, Doc, 94
Edwards, Hank, 43
Ellingsen, Bruce, 83
Elliott, Bob, 53
Ellis, John, 83, 85
Escobar, Alex, 130
Evans, Billy, 32

F
Farr, Steve, 99
Feller, Bob, 6–7, 38, 40–41, 43, 44–45, 50, 51, 53, 54, 60, 64, 68, 77, 110
Feller, Lena, 6–7
Feller, William, 6–7
Fenway Park. See Ballparks.
Fermin, Felix, 114
Fernandez, Tony, 113
Ferraro, Mike, 94
Ferrell, Rick, 34
Ferrell, Wes, 32–33, 34
Finley, Chuck, 130
Flick, Elmer, 10, 15
Fonseca, Lew, 30
Fosse, Ray, 8, 81
Foytack, Paul, 73
Francisco, Ben, 130
Franco, Julio, 111
Francona, Tito, 65, 73
Fryman, Travis, 118, 121
Fuller, Vern, 84

G
Gamble, Oscar, 84
Garcia, Dave, 94
Garcia, Mike, 60
Garko, Ryan, 130, 134–35, 138–39
Gibson, Josh, 49
Giles, Brian, 115
Glavine, Tom, 107
Goldbach, Walter, 58
Gonzalez, Juan, 126, 133
Gooden, Dwight, 68
Goodman, Billy, 43
Gordon, Joe, 47, 51, 53, 65, 69, 70
Grace, Willie, 49
Graney, Jack, 17, 59
Greenberg, Hank, 64–65, 68
Gregg, Vean, 17, 136
Grimsley, Jason, 104
Grissom, Marquis, 112
Gromek, Steve, 52–53
Grove, Lefty, 37
Guerrero, Pedro, 83

H
Hafner, Travis, 130, 132, 134–35, 136, 138–39
Hale, Odell, 35
Hall, Mel, 95
Hamilton, Tom, 59
Harder, Mel, 33, 35, 36–37, 42, 66, 99
Hargrove, Mike, 9, 91, 94, 98, 115, 124
Harrah, Toby, 9, 83
Harrelson, Ken, 82, 84
Harris, Bucky, 50
Hart, John, 94, 98, 104, 105, 114, 115, 124, 130
Hegan, Jim, 52, 60
Held, Woodie, 70, 73
Helf, Hank, 41
Hendrick, George, 84
Hershiser, Orel, 107
Heyman, Jon, 115
Hickman, Jim, 81
Hilgendorf, Tom, 78–79
Hodge, Harold "Gomer," 81
Hollinger, William, 13
Holmes, Tommy, 52
Hope, Bob, 45, 46, 74, 99
Horton, Tony, 82, 84
Houtteman, Art, 60
Howe, George W., 13
Howe, Steve, 99
Hughey, Jim, 21

I
Ingraham, Jim, 114

J
Jackson, Mike, 118
Jackson, Reggie, 93
Jackson, "Shoeless Joe," 15, 18, 25
Jacobs, David, 103
Jacobs, Richard, 102–03, 123, 124
Jacobs Field. See Progressive Field. See also Ballparks.
James, Chris, 95
Jamieson, Charlie, 30, 31
Jefferson, Reggie, 114
Jeter, Derek, 121
Jethroe, Sam, 49
John, Tommy, 67, 71, 74

143

Johnson, Ban, 19, 25
Johnson, Randy, 77, 103, 105
Jones, Harry, 59
Jones, "Sad Sam," 21
Joss, Addie, 10, 19, 76
Justice, David, 107, 112, 116, 119

K
Kaiser, David, 52
Kahn, Roger, 73
Keltner, Ken, 38, 42, 43, 51
Kennard Street Park. *See* Ballparks.
Kennedy, Doc, 13
Kent, Jeff, 111
Kilduff, Pete, 27
Killebrew, Harmon, 65, 71
Kiner, Ralph, 64–65
Kingdome. *See* Ballparks.
Kirby, Wayne, 103
Kline, Steve, 83
Knickerbocker, Bill, 35
Koenig, Mark, 31
Kouzmanoff, Kevin, 130
Kuenn, Harvey, 70, 71
Kuiper, Duane, 8, 89

L
Laffey, Aaron, 130
Lajoie, Napolean, 10, 14, 16–17, 18, 20
Landis, Kenesaw, 6, 25
Lane, Frank, 62, 64–65, 67, 69, 70, 71, 72, 80
LaPorta, Matt, 139
Lawton, Matt, 130
League Park. *See* Dunn Field. *See also* Ballparks.
Lebovitz, Hal, 77, 114
Lee, Cliff, 119, 131, 133, 134, 136, 138–39
Lemon, Bob, 43, 52–53, 54–55, 60, 65, 113
Lemon, Jim, 77
Leonard, Buck, 49
Levsen, Dutch, 31
Lewis, Franklin, 19
Lewis, Mark, 97
Leyland, Jim, 113
Lofton, Kenny, 99, 105, 112, 118, 126
Lopez, Al, 57, 60, 65
Lopez, Albie, 111
Lord, Bristol, 18
Lowenstein, John, 89
Lunte, Harry, 26
Lupica, Charlie, 54

M
Mac, Johnny, 94
Mack, Connie, 14, 18, 36
Maddux, Greg, 107
Mails, Duster, 25, 26
Malden, Karl, 69
Manning, Rick, 8–9, 89, 92
Manuel, Charlie, 126
Maris, Roger, 66, 70
Marquard, Rube, 26, 29
Martin, Billy, 65, 70, 87
Martinez, Dennis, 103, 104, 107, 112
Martinez, Victor, 124–25, 132, 134–35, 138–39
Mays, Carl, 24, 28
Mays, Willie, 60–61, 103, 120
McCormick, Jim, 13
McDougald, Gil, 68
McDowell, Jack, 111, 112
McDowell, "Sudden Sam," 62, 75, 77, 81, 86
McKean, Ed, 10–11, 13
McKechnie, Bill, 38–39
McLish, Cal, 65
McNamara, John, 94
Medich, George "Doc," 88
Memorial Stadium. *See* Ballparks.
Mesa, Jose, 104, 111, 112–13, 118
Mileti, Nick, 82
Miller, Otto, 27
Miller, Ray, 36
Miller Park. *See* Ballparks.
Minoso, Minnie, 65, 70
Mitchell, Clarence, 27
Mitchell, Dale, 44
Modell, Art, 21, 110
Morris, Jack, 93, 96, 104
Mossi, Don, 60, 65
Moyer, Jamie, 126
Mueller, Nick, 43
Municipal Stadium. *See* Cleveland Municipal Stadium. *See also* Ballparks.
Murray, Eddie, 96, 103, 111
Musial, Stan, 70

N
Nagy, Charles, 111, 113, 118, 121
Narleski, Ray, 60, 65
Neal, Bob, 59
Nettles, Graig, 76, 83
New Orleans Superdome. *See* Ballparks.

O
Ocker, Sheldon, 119
Ogea, Chad, 112–13, 118
Ojeda, Bob, 98
Olin, Patti, 98
Olin, Steve, 98
O'Neill, Steve, 22, 27, 30

P
Paige, Satchel, 7, 47, 56
Patkin, Max, 46
Paul, Gabe, 72, 83, 94
Peña, Tony, 106–07
Peralta, Jhonny, 129, 134, 139
Perkins, Anthony, 69
Perry, Gaylord, 8, 77, 82, 85, 86, 88–89, 138
Perry, Jim, 88–89
Peters, Hank, 115
Peterson, Fritz, 83
Phillips, Brandon, 119, 133
Piersall, Jimmy, 69, 70
Piniella, Lou, 126
Pluto, Terry, 99, 113
Polo Grounds. *See* Ballparks.
Posada, Jorge, 118
Powell, Boog, 8, 85
Power, Vic, 65, 70, 71
Progressive Field. *See* Jacobs Field. *See also* Ballparks.
Pytlak, Frankie, 41

R
Ramirez, Manny, 97, 118, 120, 126
Ramos, Pedro, 73
Reagan, Ronald, 54, 93
Reinert, Fred, 58
Renteria, Edgar, 113
Rhodes, Dusty, 60–61
Rice, Grantland, 20
Rickey, Branch, 133
Rincon, Ricardo, 115
Rivera, Mariano, 112
Riverfront Stadium. *See* Ballparks.
Robinson, Eddie, 51
Robinson, Frank, 8, 78, 85, 86, 88–89, 94
Robinson, Jackie, 48–49, 88
Robinson, Wilbert, 26
Robison, Frank, 13, 16, 21
Robison, Stanley, 13, 21
Rose, Pete, 81, 93, 103
Rosen, Al, 38, 49, 57, 60, 64–65, 82
Rosewater, Amy, 127
Roth, Braggo, 30
Ruth, Babe, 14, 18, 31, 37
Ryan, Nolan, 93
Ryan, Terry, 130

S
Sabathia, CC, 126, 131, 134–35, 136, 138–39
Sain, Johnny, 44, 52–53
Samuel, Marsh, 46
Scheinblum, Richie, 84
Schmidt, Mike, 93
Schneider, Russell, 49, 82, 91
Score, Herb, 59, 62–63, 64–65, 66, 68, 113, 122
Seghi, Phil, 83, 86, 89
Selby, Bill, 132
Sewell, Joe, 26, 28, 31
Sexson, Richie, 115
Shapiro, Mark, 130, 131, 132, 133, 134
Shapiro, Ron, 130
Shaute, Lefty, 30, 31
Shoppach, Kelly, 139
Siebert, Sonny, 74
Simmons, Al, 51
Sims, Duke, 84
Sipe, Brian, 93
Sizemore, Grady, 119, 124, 133, 134–35, 136, 138–39
Slapnicka, Cy, 6, 40, 68
Smiley, John, 112
Smith, Elmer, 22–23, 27, 42
Smith, Ozzie, 114
Smoltz, John, 107
Snyder, Cory, 97
Sockalexis, Louis, 13
Somers, Charles, 18, 20
Sorrento, Paul, 104
Southworth, Billy, 53
Spahn, Warren, 52–53
Speaker, Tris "The Gray Eagle," 10, 15, 19, 20–21, 22, 24, 26–27, 30, 31, 68
Spikes, Charlie, 83, 84
Steinbrenner, George, 82
Stengel, Casey, 57
Stepien, Ted, 93
Stewart, Dave, 94
Stouffer, Vernon, 82
Strickland, George, 75
Summa, Homer, 31
Sutcliffe, Rick, 95

T
Tabler, Pat, 92
Tait, Joe, 59, 87
Tavarez, Julian, 107
Thomas, Freddie, 21
Thomas, Gorman, 96
Thome, Jim, 112, 117, 118, 127, 128, 132
Thornton, Andre, 8, 90, 91
Thornton, Andy, 90
Thornton, Gertrude, 90
Thornton, Theresa, 90
Tiant, Luis, Jr., 76
Tiant, Luis, Sr., 76
Tidrow, Dick, 83
Tiger Stadium. *See* Ballparks.
Torborg, Jeff, 94
Torre, Joe, 119
Trillo, Manny, 96
Trosky, Hal, 32, 42, 50, 120
Trouppe, Quincy, 49
Trout, Dizzy, 49
Tunney, Gene, 43

U
Uhle, George, 30, 31

V
Valenzuela, Fernando, 93
Veeck, Bill, Jr., 37, 38–39, 45, 46–47, 48–49, 50, 51, 52, 55, 56, 57, 58, 65, 72, 74, 99, 106
Vernon, Mickey, 43, 57
Vitt, Oscar, 33, 42
Vizcaino, Jose, 111
Vizquel, Omar, 9, 110, 113, 114, 117, 121, 129
Voinovich, George, 103
Vosmik, Joe, 32, 37

W
Wallace, Bobby, 12
Walsh, Ed, 19
Wambsganss, Bill, 22, 27, 30, 139
Washington, Kyle, 104
Wedge, Eric, 130, 133, 138–39
Wells, David, 117
Wertz, Vic, 60, 65, 67
Westbrook, Jake, 119, 134–35, 138–39
Wheat, Zack, 26–27
White, George, 36
White, Jim "Deacon," 12
White, Michael, 103
Whitt, Ernie, 92
Wickander, Kevin, 98
Wickman, Bob, 115, 134
Williams, Matt, 112
Williams, Ted, 50, 69
Williams, Walt, 84
Winfield, Dave, 96
Wohlers, Mark, 107
Wolcott, Bob, 107
Woodling, Gene, 43
Wright, Jaret, 112–13, 117, 118
Wynn, Early, 47, 60–61, 65, 66, 73

Y
Yankee Stadium. *See* Ballparks.
Young, Cy, 10–11, 13, 14, 16, 21
Young, Dick, 85

Z
Zimmer, Chief, 10–11
Zoldak, Sam, 52